Praise for:

D0110054

Confounding the Wise

"Dan and his wife put their money where their mouth is. We don't need more people talking about Jesus, we need more people BEING Jesus. This book shows what that can look like in real time." - *Comedian Brad Stine "God's Comic"*

"Dan's heart for those with special needs is a clear reflection of his desire to know God more intimately. His selfless passion for others challenges my faith journey, and it's a joy to see this passion on every page of **Confounding the Wise**." – *Kirk Walden, President of Life Trends & Author of "The Wall"*

"Sometimes it takes a great book like this to draw us back into unfiltered humanity. **Confounding the Wise** is for people who know that real life is not found in Disneyland. It is for people who have enough soul and heart to look through the eyes of the lives of real people in a real world." - *Comedian Mike G. Williams, Author of "Men Moved to Mars," "Love Is Not a Three Letter Word," and "The Parable of the Muddy Jeep"*

"If you're up for reading a book that challenges, teaches, makes you laugh, makes you cry, encourages and inspires, - grab **Confounding the Wise** today. You'll be glad you did. But be warned: You will also be changed." - *Keith Ferrin, Founder of That You May Know Ministries*

"What is your favorite kind of story? An international thriller, a moving love story or true life adventure; this book has it all. With humility, honesty and a good dose of humor, author Dan Kulp tells the amazing story of his life and family. **Confounding the Wise** will inspire you to take a fresh look at yourself and this world through the eyes of God who loves to confound the wise with the people He chooses and the people He uses." – *Comedian Gordon Douglas*

"With tremendous self-effacing humor, Dan tells the story of the arduous, bureaucratic ordeal that is the international adoption of children with special needs. His approach is both comedic and challenging. As children of an adoptive Father, he explains, we ought to open ourselves to imitating that facet of our Father's love. Dan doesn't sugar-coat the difficulties, but he also demonstrates that children with special needs give more than they take. Pick up **Confounding the Wise**, and see just how this "foolish" man gets it right." - *Dr. Marc Newman, President, Speaker for Life*

"By opening up his life to us in **Confounding the Wise**, Dan Kulp educates, inspires and entertains. I enjoyed an honest, convicting glimpse into a world that many only see from the outside."- *Bill Griffin, Guitarist for The Dig Project*

"In Dan Kulp's **Confounding the Wise** you are brought on a journey that plucks at your heart strings and challenges your perception and treatment of both orphans and especially people with special needs." – *Mike Higgins, Lead Guitarist for The Dig Project*

"If you want an honest look at adoption and life with children with special needs, this book is a beautiful example. The world needs more people like Dan (and his wife!) to step up and love these kids. Dan's commitment to bringing orphans home rings true in every aspect of his life." – *Jeff Norsen, Bass Player for The Dig Project*

"It's cool that I know Dan, because I can attest that his passion and love for the Lord and his family that comes across in this book is true. I hope that people who are thinking about adopting or facing struggles in the process will be encouraged by the story of what God has done in the Kulp family." – *Dave Hopping of Comedians Dave and Brian*

"Since meeting Dan Kulp back in 2010, I've told a brief recap of his story hundreds of times and it's always been met with awe and inspiration, but after reading **Confounding the Wise** a couple of weeks ago, and learning 'the rest of the story,' I am as committed as ever to making sure thousands more hear Dan and Elizabeth's story in hopes they'll respond with the same passion to those small voices who ask for so little of us, and who have so much to give." – *Dana Ashley, Artist Representative for Ambassador Speakers Bureau*

"I read this book when I was supposed to be writing a sermon. Couldn't put it down. And you won't be able to put it down either. Dan's story is remarkable. Dan's wife is remarkable. And despite his protests to the contrary, so is Dan." - *Pastor Jeff Long, Farmington UMC*

"This book will inspire you to look back through your life journey and see the promise of Jeremiah 29:11: 'I know the plans I have for you, declares the Lord...' It will also show you the importance of a father's example in loving his children and valuing all life. Dan's book is passionate and honest." – *T.K. Kennedy, Young Life Area Director, Long Island*

"This is a poignant description of ministry, compassion, understanding and the determination of one family to be in the Lord's service. Children with special needs are not always given to those who are both willing and able to meet their needs. But here we discover there are people who will seek sacrifice in order to provide the life that so many are willing to discard. **Confounding the Wise** describes the sometimes brutal view that many countries have toward Down syndrome and other diagnoses. Herein also is the story of unconditional love for children who so desperately need those who are willing to give it. – *Brian Callahan, President of the Flower City Down Syndrome Network*

"It was better than *Cats.*" – *Dan Kulp*

Confounding the Wise

A Celebration of Life, Love, Laughter, Adoption
and the Joy of Children with Special Needs

Confounding the Wise

A Celebration of Life, Love, Laughter, Adoption
and the Joy of Children with Special Needs

by

DAN KULP

Brian,
Many blessings!
Dan John 10:10

WordCrafts

Published by WordCrafts Press
Tullahoma, TN 37388
www.wordcrafts.net

In Memory of Norm Kulp

November 15, 1937 - March 3, 2014

"But God hath chosen the foolish things of the world to confound the wise; and God hath chosen the weak things of the world to confound the things which are mighty."

1 Corinthians 1:27

The woods where Simon was found.

Contents

Author's Note

For as far back as I can remember, the accepted standard of language usage in regards to the developmentally challenged is always changing. For example, trisomy 21, a condition by which someone has an extra 21st chromosome (or a 3rd copy), used to be called Down's Syndrome – named after Dr. Down, the person who discovered this trait. In the United States, the widely accepted description is currently Down syndrome - without the apostrophe and with a lower case s on the word syndrome. While I have chosen to use this term, or Ds throughout the book, I'm sure someone, somewhere, someday will tell all of us that there is an even more acceptable way to say it.

In honor of my siblings and son - David, Matthew, Sarah, Suzanne and Simon - I have included an extra 21st chapter.

While this story is true, some names have been changed to protect privacy.

"Why any kid would want to be an orphan is beyond me."
Miss Hannigan
Annie, 1977

Introduction

I am haunted by an image in my mind of a lone figure walking toward me on a busy street in the city of Guangzhou, China.

I stopped dead in my tracks and stared in his direction until I could be sure. Perhaps it was because his gait was a familiar sight to me, or something about his movements. Whatever it was, I had a strong feeling that this person heading in my direction had Down syndrome. As I waited for him to get close enough to confirm my theory, I noticed he was stopping every few yards, at the garbage cans which lined the street. He would look down and inspect the container and then continue along the sidewalk. When he finally got close enough for me to make eye contact, I was struck by how filthy he was, covered from head to toe with dirt and grime. I soon guessed that he was homeless and had been searching the garbage cans for a meal. His hair was long and greasy. The truth is I didn't know if this person, who was probably in his early twenties, was a male or female until the very moment he stood in front of me.

Through the grime, tattered clothing and the unkempt hair came the most beautifully warm smile, as he looked at me looking at him. The smile reminded me of so many people with Down syndrome I have met all over the United States, throughout my life. In this young man's eyes I saw my brothers David and Matthew, and sisters Suzanne and Sarah, as well as my son Simon.

I attempted to communicate with him and express that I was a friend. He was receptive and seemed rather delighted that I was relating to him. To the people in his society, I had the feeling he was invisible at best, and a reviled outcast at worst.

I was holding bottled water which I gave to him and once again his bright smile shined like the sun. Street vendors were beginning to take notice now and were wondering why this American was taking such an interest in one of their disposable members of society. One young lady who knew a little English came up to me and asked me why I was being nice to the homeless man. I tried to explain that my son was Chinese and had Down syndrome. I even pointed to a tattoo of Simon's name on my arm, written in Chinese, and said "Simon is like him" while I pointed in my new friend's direction. She was still confused. I asked her if she would take a picture of the two of us. Soon, a small crowd had gathered and there was a buzz in the air. I wanted to spend more time with my new acquaintance but I feared I was creating a spectacle and didn't want that for him. I said goodbye to the homeless man as he proudly showed off his bottle of clean, fresh water.

I regret not having bought him a meal. In my haste to not draw too much attention to the situation, I hadn't even thought of it. There were food vendors everywhere. I wish I had provided him with the most robust meal he had ever eaten.

As I made my way back to an indoor shopping center where my wife, in-laws and newly adopted daughter were, the thought suddenly hit me that the fate of my children may have been the same as the street person whom I had just met. Would Simon, if not adopted, have been turned out of the orphanage when he was eighteen? I shudder to think of him or Danielle being left to fend for themselves for food, clothing and shelter. I cringe as I wonder how easily they could become victims to those who would seek to do them harm. The gravity of what we were doing in China for a second time hit me with such clarity. We were adopting because all children should have a Mommy and a Daddy.

I started writing this book about five years ago. Much has happened in my life between writing the first page and the last. The most significant thing is that my father passed away. Even though I will not be able to hand him his very own copy, as you will soon read, his fingerprints are all over this book.

It occurred to me that when my mom passes away someday, I will be like an orphan. What a strange thought. I can be quite glad however, that my experience is not like that of a child abandoned at a mall, train station or hotel. Or one raised in an orphanage and owned by the state, or the homeless young man with Down syndrome I met living on the streets. I had a mom and dad who were there for me for most of my life, and for that, I am eternally grateful.

I didn't write **Confounding the Wise** out of any sort of arrogance, as if my life is so important you just needed to read all about it. If you say to yourself at any time, "Wow!" while reading this, understand that I do the same thing. I am utterly blown away by the story God has given me to live. He was preparing me from the time I was a child for the family I have today. We've been told Simon is the first child who has Down syndrome to be adopted out of China to the United States. I'm truly amazed. Out of all the parents in the world God could have chosen for Simon, He chose us.

When I dream, I dream big. I hope when you read this, you will be inspired in the same way I was when my wife came home from China after her first trip and shared her story with me. I want loads of people to read this and be challenged to adopt a child. I would love for people to see clearly within these pages the joy children with special needs can bring to one's life. It would be great, too, if it opened people's hearts to the value of life.

With all of this in mind, "Confounding the Wise" is dedicated to people like my wife and parents, to orphans, to those in life affirming ministries, to caregivers and teachers of those with special needs, to adoptive families all around the world, and for those who "get" why this book has an extra twenty-first chapter.

While I've dedicated it to them, it is for you. Yes, you. No matter who you are. I'm dreaming that something inspires you. Moves you. Challenges you to adopt or to support those who adopt. Causes you to volunteer for a special needs organization. I don't know. Whatever it is, I hope that you will someday be able to think about your own story and say, "Wow."

Thanks for reading. I am honored.

Confounding the Wise

A Celebration of Life, Love, Laughter, Adoption
and the Joy of Children with Special Needs

1

Another Man's Treasure

There he was. Lying in the woods, in the middle of winter, on the day he was born. Alone, helpless and left to die. My wife is far less cynical than I am. She would like to believe his mother lovingly placed him there knowing with certainty he would be found by some nearby workers. I, on the other hand, can't help but think that the woman who had just given birth to her child decided to have a post pregnancy abortion. She left him not for someone to find and turn into the proper authorities. She left him to die from exposure and eventually be covered with snow. Or perhaps the woman's husband, unhappy with the child's physical deformities, forced her to abandon him or took the newborn himself into the woods. Either way, this was day one in the life of one of my most treasured prizes, Simon, my son.

Simon was born on December 28th, 2004. He probably wasn't abandoned because he had Down syndrome, a genetic mutation having to do with an extra 21st chromosome. This would probably not have been visible or familiar to his parents so soon after his birth. He was most likely taken to those woods because of more obvious physical characteristics. Simon had a club foot, an imperforate anus (an internal abnormality in which the intestines doesn't connect to an exit) and an extra thumb on his left hand. To a culture that finds imperfection shameful or embarrassing, these traits would be reason enough for a parent to get rid of him. Thank God they failed. In fact, I believe God is completely responsible for my son's survival. I am reminded of a statement by Joseph in the Old Testament, who would one day say to those who had abandoned him, "You intended to harm me, but God intended it for good."

Simon did not perish that cold winter day. He was found by a man named Mr. Han who was hired by a landowner in the province of Hebei, China, to help clear the woods of downed branches and other debris before springtime. Surprised by the discovery of the newborn, Mr. Han and his wife quickly brought the baby to a nearby shack where they warmed him up and kept good care of the little life until they were able to bring the infant to a police station several hours later. Mr. Han was impressed by the infants' strength as evidenced by his lack of crying from the cold and hunger.

Elizabeth and I would not learn of little Simon until about two years later. Through a miraculous set of circumstances, he would one day be ours.

2

Recalling the Crazies

I learned a couple of things when I stepped off that plane in China. The first thing I learned was that I was the fattest guy in all of China! My wife is tall, thin and pretty. Together we must have looked like the number ten roaming around the countryside.

The second thing I learned was that it is not impolite to stare in the Chinese culture. We were stared at everywhere we went. Not only because I was the fattest guy in all of China, but also because, by day two of our trip, we had our new son in our arms. This was bothersome to many because we had a boy. It is much more common for westerners to adopt Chinese girls, and is therefore a more familiar sight. Simon's special needs got him onto the waiting child list. These needs are not clearly visible, and if the onlookers knew, instead of being angry they would be completely baffled as to why we would want him.

So there we were, sitting in restaurants and touring the sites, all the while being closely observed by the general public. My wife was annoyed by it all. At first, I felt like a rock star. I pretended I was Bono and that everyone around me was captivated by my mere presence. However, by week two, I felt the strain of the stares as well. I can remember one particular day, sitting in a hotel restaurant with Liz and

Simon, feeling the weight of dozens of leers. Something wonderful happened. I remembered. A flashback. Things I hadn't thought of for years. Memories flooded back to me.

My adoption journey began long before we were matched with an adorable little boy from Hebei, China. Mine began in March of 1971. I was originally the fifth child born to Norm and Carol Kulp. Five kids and they weren't even Catholic! I'm not sure if they planned it this way or not, but they sure did things right. First there was Linda, then Chris and Steve, all born about a year apart from each other. A couple years behind them was Lori. And eleven years after their first, I was born. By this time, my folks had free babysitting, mostly from Linda.

Not content to stop with me, on March 26th, 1971, my brother Matthew was born. Shortly after his birth, the doctor told my dad that Matthew was Mongoloid (an outdated term used to describe Down syndrome). My father didn't know what that meant so he had to look it up in a dictionary. After learning the definition and sharing this new diagnosis with others, many told Dad the same thing: put him in an institution, get rid of him and forget he was ever born. Well, this didn't sit well with my folks. In fact, years later, in a television interview, my dad said he felt "that the Lord has given Matthew to us, he has chosen us to take Matthew, that was the way it was gonna be."

So they did. Matthew was a full-fledged member of the Kulp family. We didn't find out until years later that the very name "Matthew" means "Gift from God". And he certainly was. In fact, Matthew was such a blessing to the family, my parents made the radical decision to adopt three more children, all of whom had Down syndrome!

So this was my life growing up. My parents were the neighborhood weirdos and I was one of their nine kids! This was the 1970s. Nobody kept kids who were different. At the very least, you didn't flaunt them and you certainly didn't go out and get more!

We were considered such an oddity that occasionally a spotlight of media attention shined on our family. Newspaper articles and TV interviews came about every once in a while. In fact, on November 24th, 1980, we were included in a PBS/Newsweek documentary called "Cover Story: Adoption in America", which aired all over the world. It was a thrill in fourth grade to have a crew come to our house for a few days and film our family. I used to talk about the experience at show and tell. What an annoying kid I must have been.

Things got even stranger when there was a two page spread about us in 1981 in the "National Enquirer." The "National Enquirer!" This wasn't the "National Enquirer" of today, filled with stories about Brad and Angelina. This was the Enquirer of the early eighties, with features like "Two Headed Alien Gives Birth to Human Child." And, oh yeah, the Kulp family! I can remember my parents arguing about who was going to walk down to the corner store and pick up twelve copies to hand out only to close relatives and friends. We lived in the small Mayberry-like town of Honeoye Falls, N.Y., and knew that as soon as one of us walked out of that old fashioned drug store with those rags, it wouldn't be long before the whole town knew about it.

In addition to some media coverage, we also got stares. A lot of stares. Everywhere we went, people gawked at us. And I'm not talking about the spectacle of seeing a family of eleven trounce around the area. Most of the time it was just me, Matt and the three adopted children, David, Suzanne and Sarah. The older ones had either moved on to build their own lives or they were about to. I'm the one who received both the blessing and the challenge of growing up amongst four brothers and sisters with special needs.

Dad: Why Be Normal?

In many ways, my Dad and I are very much alike. We both have a very pronounced receding hairline. As someone who has been immersed in the rock band culture for the past several years, this is especially disturbing to me. Everyone knows that rockers have great hair. Rockers, except for me that is. I must admit I often find myself cursing my own head when I see other bands on stage, with musicians who can do really cool things with their hair. Not only do they do really cool things with their hair, but they do really cool things in several different ways. I feel the weight of my cursed head on my shoulders with bands I especially like because I will attend their shows multiple times, and at each concert the musicians look a little different. I have to settle for varying degrees of shortness. My alternatives are short and very short. I often opt for the almost bald look because, if I don't, my widow's peak sticks out and I end up looking like an older, overweight version of Eddie Munster. Thanks Dad!

I think, too, I must have inherited my physique from him. My father is in his mid-seventies now. He actually looks great. Very svelte. However, I have seen his eleven sisters and most of them were shaped like me. Our family reunions looked like Liberty Bell conventions. Thanks again, Dad!

Hairline and body type aside, there is one far more significant similarity between Dan and Norm Kulp. We both love to laugh. My dad has a great sense of humor. He is a very funny guy. Making people laugh is great, but what I think we both share is a love of laughter itself. I have many joys in life - looking at my children as they lay peacefully asleep in their beds, praise from my wife, movies, and food (ahem) are just a few. Without a doubt, in my top ten has to be making my father laugh. I love saying just the right thing that puts that grin on his face from ear to ear and makes his shoulders shake up and down as he howls straight from his gut. When this happens, I feel like I hit the jackpot at a slot machine. Thanks yet again, Dad, for I am convinced that laughter is one of many wonderful gifts from God. After spending time with my family one holiday evening, a friend of mine told me he noticed how much we all laughed together. He also told me his family never really did that growing up. I couldn't imagine.

So as much as we are alike, we are also very different. For example, growing up, I was convinced my dad could fix just about everything. If the space shuttle ever crashed landed outside our house on Monroe Street in Honeoye Falls, I could picture him heading outside with his tool box in hand. "Pop the hood!" he would yell up to the astronaut. And, with his plumbers' crack in plain sight, Dad would start working on it.

I don't remember a repairman ever coming to the Kulp household because whatever it was that needed fixing, Dad would get his tool box. If the TV was on the fritz, he would pull that giant console away from the wall and begin surgery. If it could be carried downstairs to his workbench, he would work on it down there.

Now that I am a father I realize why this may have been ideal for him. It would be his only refuge in a home with many kids. The only place where he could get some peace. Like the patriarch in the movie "A Christmas Story", sometimes we would even hear that "tapestry of obscenity" that "is still hanging in space over Lake Michigan" (although in our case, it would be Lake Ontario) when things were obviously not going his way in the repair world. Also, like the father in the famous Christmas tale, it wasn't exactly discernible curse words, as my dad's harshest and favorite was the phrase "Dumb, stupid!" well-placed before the object of his wrath (i.e. "Dumb, stupid furnace!" or "Dumb, stupid car!").

I did not receive his gift of handiness. I can't fix anything. If something breaks around my home the best I can do is pick up a phone and call someone who can. That is, of course, unless my wife hasn't already fixed it, as she is far handier than I. My brother Steve did inherit Dad's abilities; he is one of the most talented handymen I know. In fact, Steve is everything I am not - tall, thin, muscular and rugged. One macho, cool dude. He, like our father, can also fix anything. Sometimes that phone call goes out to him.

Admittedly, I don't call Steve nearly as much as I should. This is for no other lame reason than the busyness of life, which allows days to turn into months without calling. It is quite alright; he does the same thing. Steve is actually one of my heroes in this life, but my reminder to call happens to be when something around our home breaks. Then I am in the uncomfortable position of not wanting to be the guy that only calls when he needs something, while really needing my brother to help me out. So, I usually call and make small talk and slip in the fact that our (fill in the blank here) is on the outs and I am not sure what to do. He is a good man, though, and always offers to come over and "take a look," even though he is quite busy with his own life, I am sure. After the required rounds of, "Oh, you don't have to do that" and "No, it's no problem", I give in and set that appointment for my big brother to come over and not only make the diagnosis, but also fix the darn the thing.

It becomes more awkward because, even after all of these years of free house calls from Steve, I still am not sure what I am supposed to do while he is working. Do I just stand there for five hours as he works on our hot water heater? I think it is probably rude to go watch TV. But really, having me just stand there and hover over him doesn't seem that great for either of us. At times I even feel like a five-year-old as I hand him a tool from his tool box every now and then. Sometimes I tell him the same joke when he's finished - "Thanks Steve, maybe I can come over to your house and sing for you and the family some time." He has saved me thousands of dollars over my lifetime. And what have I given him? Lame jokes. Pretty inequitable, if you ask me.

Back to Dad. Another stark contrast between my father and I is that he just likes to blend in. He doesn't want to stand out in a crowd. In fact, he doesn't really like crowds at all. I, on the other hand, have chosen paths that have been very public. Throughout my school days, I was always involved in the musicals, theater, chorus, etc. Even now, I am an actor, writer and comedian. I am the lead singer for a touring rock band called The Dig Project that has performed all over the U.S. I even hosted a call-in radio show for teens. These are all very public roles in which I am often the center of attention. Dad could care less about any of that. He would much rather be in the background.

He doesn't like being embarrassed either. I can remember the year he stopped letting me go with him for our annual tradition of cutting down the Christmas tree together. I was in my late teens and we went to the same tree farm we had been going to for my entire life. After hiking around for several minutes over snow covered hills and in between many majestic evergreens, we found The One. Each year at Christmas time, our home always had the most perfectly shaped tree. This particular year would be no exception. For some reason, though, as soon as the blade of Dad's saw touched the trunk, I thought it would be funny to yell over and over again, "Oh no! Please don't harm this beautiful tree!" like I was some sort of environmentalist tree hugger. With Dad sprawled out on the ground with his head stuck under the lower boughs of the pine, and me standing there with mock tears amongst several curious onlookers, I was told in a not so Christmassy voice to "SHUT UP!"

When we arrived home, my mom asked how the trip went. Dad informed her that I would never be going with him again. And I didn't. At least for a couple more years until he finally gave in and decided, with a warning for me to never do that again, that we should reboot our tradition.

One of my many favorite stories to share about my dad has to do with a father/son bake auction to benefit my Boy Scout Troop. The auction was to take place on a Wednesday afternoon at a pavilion in Mendon Ponds Park, near our home. The troop had hired a professional auctioneer to come and auction off bake goods produced by each scout and his father.

My dad loved peanut butter cookies. They were amongst his favorite treats. Shortly before the bake auction, he found a new recipe he had never tried before. Convinced that this concoction would outdo all others, he decided these were the cookies we would bake and therefore impress anyone lucky enough to bid and win them. So, after his Tuesday night television ritual, Dad rolled off the couch at about 9:00 pm and said, "Come on, let's go bake those cookies." For the next hour and a half, we mixed ingredients, shaped dough and baked revolutionary peanut butter delights. One problem - we never once tasted the cookies to see how we were doing. Late at night and after several batches, Dad handed one to me and at the same time we each took a bite. They were the worst cookies we had ever tasted in our lives! I'm not sure if we had screwed something up or if the recipe was completely illegitimate. There was no time for that now. The auction was in less than twenty hours!

After the initial shock of what just entered our mouths, Dad quickly formulated a plan. We would go to the park the next day and bid on our own submission. We would win the cookies and dispose of them and no one would know of our failure. It would be a small and patriotic price to pay for supporting Troop 664 of the Boy Scouts of America.

The next day, I sat with my parents and my siblings David, Sarah, Suzanne and Matthew at a picnic table underneath the pavilion. The auctioneer was fun to listen to as he spoke really fast and sold a variety of brownies, cookies, cakes and pies to the highest bidder. Each plate went for about three or four dollars. When it came time to auction our awful contribution, my father elbowed me to raise my arm up high and start the bidding. In a strange twist of events, a family down at the other end of the picnic table saw this exchange occur between my dad and me. Now, I'm not sure if they thought we had some sort of insider trading information on this particular baked goodie, but the other dad elbowed his kid to also raise his hand. We got into a bidding war with this other family! When the twelve dollar mark was reached, my Dad grabbing my arm and speaking softly out of the side of his mouth said, "Forget it. We're not paying twelve bucks for those cookies. They're horrible!" He let the other family win our disgusting donation!

Immediately following the event, while all of the other scouts were running around the playground and comparing merit badges, etc., Dad was ushering our family into the station wagon and peeling out of the parking lot, hoping not to be discovered as the wretched baker.

Another example of shunning a spotlight: Dad hated bumper stickers because he thought they drew too much attention to one's car. He even complained about others on the road who had bumper stickers on the rear of their automobile. He would refuse such idiocy. That is until about my senior year of high school. I can still remember him coming home all excited because he had found a bumper sticker worth slapping on the back of his pickup truck. He felt it perfectly described our entire family. For all of the stares and unwanted attention, bad advice from people who told him what he should do with his "Mongoloid" kid and huge family filled with nine children, all with very distinct foibles and personalities, Dad had found an answer which to him seemed to sum it all up. The sticker read "WHY BE NORMAL?"

4

Mom Loves Black People!

While Dad kept food on the table and a roof over our heads, I have to believe my mother was a driving force when it came to the adoptions and the raising of their children. How do I know this? Because quite frankly, I am a dad now myself. I know from experience that, left to the raising of my kids on my own (God forbid), our family unit would be filled with noise, clutter, chaos and a complete lack of focus. I would have absolutely no idea how to fight certain battles on behalf of my kids, nor would I even know there were battles to be fought. Simon would attend school with the same shirt three days in a row (if it passed the "sniff" test), and Danielle would probably never wear her glasses, because I would forget that she had glasses to wear. As Jim Carrey's character in the film "Bruce Almighty" so aptly stated, "Behind every great man there's a woman rolling her eyes".

Enter my mom. Like my own wife, she is everything a mother should be. In fact, I would venture to say my mother is a combination of the best qualities shared by great TV moms like June Cleaver, Carol Brady and Shirley Partridge…with an edge.

Carol Kulp has never been one to back down, give up or shut up. She speaks the truth with the wisdom and firmness of one made confident by possessing a spiritual strength. My memories of her growing up are a pleasant mix of tenderness and toughness, calmness and courage.

Most in our family would say that I inherited my ability to sing from Mom. Our house was often filled with the sound of Mom's soprano voice belting out tunes like "Blessed Assurance" and "How Great Thou Art". In the summertime, when all of the windows in our non-air-conditioned house were open, several neighbors were also treated to her beautiful songs of praise.

As a singer too, I was not the first to catch her spirit of song. My brother Matthew's favorite tune of all time was "It's a Small World". I think it caught his attention on one of our vacations to Disney World in Florida. The colorful ride consisted of a boat journey through a variety of scenes featuring mechanical children representing every tribe and nation, singing in unison the words "It's a small world after all." Matthew was hooked! Soon after, he was given a 45 record with the same song. Matt now would belt it out at the top of his lungs so the rest of the "small world" could listen, too.

I'm not sure what it is, as I am not an expert on the psychology of Down syndrome (just a fan), but there is something about that extra chromosome which makes one extremely content with repetition, habit and familiarity. I mean, there are millions of great songs, kid! Would it have killed him to spin some Elvis, R.E.O. Speedwagon or Billy Joel? Heck, I would have settled for the theme to Scooby Doo just to hear something different. Nope. "It's a Small World."

Eventually, someone came up with the idea of giving Matt a set of headphones. And while we and the rest of our neighborhood still had to hear his enthusiastic bellows, at least we no longer had to hear the same song over and over, because, for the most part, Matthews' rendition was fairly unrecognizable without the recording to back him up. I'm glad our town was savvy enough to know it was Matthew and not some sort of moaning poltergeist living in our hundred and fifty year old house. For the record, I say this with much affection, as the memories of the sound of my brothers' voice, along with my mother's own beautiful singing, brings much joy to my mind and heart.

Diversity is a passion of my mother's. What I mean to say is, my mom loves black people! Ever since I can remember, she has had a fondness for black culture. She smiles when she hears urban street lingo and thinks Queen Latifah is a hoot. In fact, recently, she told me about how, for supper one night, she and my father skipped their local Arby's and went to one closer to the inner city of Rochester. She was more than delighted being the only white people in the restaurant.

I say Mom loves black people, but in all fairness Mom just loves people. When all of us kids were in school and she had a little more time on her hands, she worked various part time jobs to supplement the family income. She worked as a lunch room monitor in the high school. She helped clean the house of an upper class ailing widow. Eventually, Mom began working as a paraprofessional in a social work type situation for a program called Visiting Friends. Her responsibility was to build relationships with other mothers in some of our areas most run-down and crime stricken neighborhoods in order to help them navigate some of life's challenges. Although only in high school at the time, I shared my Dad's concerns for her safety. It was tough to imagine Mom being in the hood and entering apartment complexes everyday inhabited by drug dealers, parolees and, quite frankly, people who often look at Caucasians as the enemy. Despite our concerns, she stuck to her guns and continued on in her work until she felt her time in that job was finished. I must also add that she had never been victimized in that setting either.

Many of the families she served in the city came to adore her. And she loved them back. Recently, I came across a photo that must have been of one of her clients. It was a picture of Mom in a warm embrace with a black woman and both were grinning from ear to ear. On the back was written, "You're not just my visiting friend, but you're a true friend. Love ya, Rosa and Family." Never condescending and always firm in her truth telling, Mom simply valued the lives of others. For her, joy could be found on the faces and in the stories of anyone and everyone. Whether she came home from working with that wealthy widow in the country, the mischievous teenagers in the lunchroom or a welfare mom from the ghetto, Mom would share their stories with us at the dinner table, all from the same perspective - these lives were valuable and worthy of dignity and respect.

In the schools of my small town of Honeoye Falls, N.Y., it was alarming to my mother that there seemed to be only three black students in all of the grades. So in fifth grade she enrolled me in the "Urban-Suburban Program". This is where students from the city of Rochester would be bussed to a mostly white suburban school for their education, and I would be bussed to Rochester City School #3. She wanted me to be surrounded by a much more diverse crowd of students so that I could become a more well-rounded individual. She also wanted to support my interest in acting, and School #3 had a drama class for fifth graders. She was appalled one day when she went to attend a school assembly, and she saw all of the white kids sitting on one side of the auditorium and all of the black kids sitting on the other. She felt as if her goals of diversity had been thwarted.

I am certain there is a sociological message in this, but I am not sure that it has anything to do with racism. At least not in the "I hate you because of your color" sort of definition of racism. I have noticed when groups of people gather, human beings tend to gravitate towards others with whom we are comfortable. For example, have you ever been to a graduation party for the son or daughter of a fellow church member? In a setting like this, where there is a wide mix of relatives, neighbors, friends and co-workers, where do you sit?

I was working as an Outreach Director for my home church when I discovered this phenomenon. One of my emphases was to challenge people in our congregation to reach out to others in simple ways during segregated settings. Not only was I not super successful in this cause, I found that I myself was guilty of the same behavior. Whether at a backyard barbecue or a church potluck, a birthday party or sales seminar, we tend to enter a room and gravitate towards those we know. People we are friends with. Those who allow us to be comfortable. The problem is, some are left in the dust. This can mark the difference, too, between good churches and bad. Good churches keep on the lookout for the loner or new couple who walk through their doors. Oblivious churches pay no attention and the newcomer walks away disconnected and diminished. Bill Hybels, in his book *Just Walk Across the Room*, tackles this very issue and describes how the simple act of reaching out can change people's lives. What does all of this have to do with Carol Kulp you ask?

Let's just say my mother is a Just Walk Across the Room sort of person.

In advocating for the special needs community, it can become easy to get sidetracked by causes which may not enhance the world's view towards those with physical or mental challenges. My mother had a very simple method for helping break down walls. Instead of protesting the teasers or the bullies, she knew exposure was key. I am convinced, without having any scientific data or research to back this up, that people who are in the business of making fun of others who are different in some way haven't spent enough time rubbing elbows with the subjects of their mockery.

Each year while I was in high school, a wonderful Home Ec teacher named Mrs. Bellanca would invite me, my brother and my mother to one of her classes to talk about Down syndrome. She would allow the students to ask questions. Matthew was happy to be the center of attention. When Mom would describe some of the physical characteristics of Ds, like the difference in the lifelines on their hands (people with Ds sometimes have a very pronounced singular line, called a palmar crease, across the palm of one or both of their hands, rather than two non-intersecting lines like most typical people), Matt would proudly raise his hand for the whole class to see. My fellow classmates seemed to enjoy the experience too.

From every moronic stand-up comedian who thinks it's funny to make Special Olympians the butt of their jokes to the average kid on the playground who uses the word "retard" as an insult, I believe the cure for their foolishness is to allow them the blessing of having a real life relationship with someone who is "different". The same holds true for racists. It would be hard, I think, to hold true racism in your heart towards someone of another race if you have lots of exposure to that particular race in a real life, friendly situation. Mom believed that too, and never missed an opportunity to introduce Matthew, David, Suzanne and Sarah to the rest of the world. Exposure was key.

I started stand-up comedy pretty young. After attending a city school in fifth grade and being inspired by great men and women in history like George Washington Carver, Martin Luther King Jr. and Rosa Parks, I had a noble vision for my life. A few days into the sixth grade, back in my suburban school, my teacher (Mr. Kirwin - one of my favorites) went around the room and asked each of us to tell what we wanted to be when we grew up. When it got to me, I proudly declared, "I want to be the first black President." The class erupted in laughter. Mr. K even left the room to tell fellow teachers what I just said. It became a running joke throughout the year. I can honestly say my mother never tried to hinder my dreams either. To this day, I still feel like I am in the running as Obama is really the first half-black President of the United States.

5

Elizabeth

While it could be said that my adoption journey began when my brother Matthew was born in 1970, my wife's began much later.

During our dating years, Elizabeth and I were very much an on again off again item. Deb, Elizabeth's Maid of Honor at our wedding, said in her toast that we "had more time outs than a Buffalo Bills game." When Elizabeth was ready to be married, I wasn't. When I was ready, she was unsure. I had finally gotten used to being single and enjoyed all of the perks of the lifestyle. I liked doing what I wanted, when I wanted to do it. The freedom of being a single man in his early thirties had become addictive. In my early twenties, I had been married for five years. It didn't end well. My first wife had been my first long term girlfriend and when my marriage to her ended, I was pretty devastated.

After a long time of healing, God had finally brought peace to my life. A funny thing happened at that moment too: something changed in me that gave me a confidence that must have been much more attractive to the opposite sex. I mean, I wasn't what I would call a real catch. Despite being overweight and balding, once I had gotten over the loneliness of divorce, I had started dating more than I ever had before. Being the lead singer of a pretty cool touring indie rock band didn't hurt either. I was hesitant to give up the feminine strokes to my ego. Each time she offered an ultimatum, I got scared. She is a dignified woman and not one to tolerate my shenanigans.

Elizabeth's hesitations came from a different place. While I needed to get "dating" out of my system, she was ready to settle down, be married, have a white picket fence, two-point-five kids and a husband with a nine-to-five job. Unfortunately, like I said, I am the lead singer of a rock band. Although we're not famous or signed to a major label, we had been able to maintain a pretty decent calendar of shows all across the country and we toured as much as we could. We were able to make it into some major festivals every year, to the point that we had some name recognition and felt our music careers were at least headed in the right direction. The question Elizabeth asked herself was, "Do I really want to be married to a man that will be gone on the road for much of the year?"

Whenever we both agreed that a break in our relationship was in order, she used it to pray and reflect and seek God's will in her life. I used it to meet more women. At one point, she had gotten so angry at my non-committal attitude, she literally traveled to the other side of the world just to get away. I suppose this is the effect I have on the ladies!

It was during one of these breaks when Elizabeth decided she wanted to do something different with her life. She felt the tug of God on her heart to use her skills as a physical therapist for something greater than a paycheck. Through some research and leading from the Holy Spirit, she found herself heading to an orphanage in inland China.

Although not an "official couple" at that time, Elizabeth and I maintained a close friendship. I was privileged enough, along with her mom, dad and Aunt Debbie, to be able to see her off on her big trip to China. I was completely and utterly fascinated by this woman, who would give up everything she knew and was comfortable with, for children she had never met in another country on the other side of the world. I watched as she stood in the airport, wearing her red striped shirt and pack on her back, saying goodbye to her closest loved ones. I watched as she went through security and made her way down to the end of a very long aisle towards her gate. I couldn't take my eyes off of her as she got smaller and smaller in my sight. And I remember thinking, "This is the strongest woman I have ever met."

While overseas, Elizabeth enjoyed discovering a whole new world. A different language and culture gave her much to learn about. Blending in wasn't really an option for her though, as she is quite tall and Caucasian. She would be easily spotted as a foreigner. During her free time from her work, she would go to local market places, go site seeing or sit and attempt to communicate with the locals.

When you're a stranger in a strange land the feeling of isolation may easily set in, but Elizabeth's faith in God and confidence in her mission kept her strong. Every once in a while, when discouragement or struggles set in, a call home to her mother Kathy would usually help put her back on track. Her mom, a faith filled Christian herself, was a terrific sounding board, reminding her of God's calling to the children of China.

Prior to her leaving the country, during one of our "on" times, Elizabeth and I would often sit in a beautiful park across the street from her apartment in Canandaigua, NY. Time passed quickly as we had long discussions about everything under the sun. We shared many of our hopes and dreams for the future, and surprisingly for someone with ADD, I never tired of my conversations with Elizabeth.

One particularly interesting get-to-know-you type game Elizabeth often initiates is Would You Rather? It's a simple game; she would ask me to choose between two different scenarios. When I finished answering, I then got to ask the next question. Hers were usually legitimately interesting questions which would provide some insight into the type of man I am. Things like, "Would you rather live in a big city or a small town?," "Would you rather live without eyesight or hearing?" or, "Would you rather make lots of money but have to work doing something you only somewhat enjoy, or make less money doing something you love?" If these were "maybe someday in the far off future potential husband" interviews, I suppose I answered to her satisfaction.

My questions to her were usually more comical or somewhat twisted, like "Would you rather get head lice or bed bugs?" or "If someone broke into your home, would you rather shoot them in the head or in the stomach?" Like I said, twisted. I remember one question I asked her was, "Would you rather find out I was a closet druggie or an assassin for the government?" I clarified this by explaining I only took out evil dictators and such as a Jack Bauer style agent. A lively but friendly discussion ensued as she insisted she much preferred I was addicted to illicit drugs rather than a taker of human life. "But I would be ridding the world of evil people! I could actually be saving thousands of lives by ending just one," I protested. She could not be convinced.

After she had left for China, I was fortunate enough to speak with her once in a while by phone. I enjoyed these brief moments as she described her daily events, cultural discoveries and sites she had seen. One particular conversation stands out to me now as I reflect back on those phone calls. Elizabeth had reminded me of our Would You Rather game in the park a few weeks prior. She asked if I remembered the question about me ridding the world of evil people in order to save lives. I told her I remembered. "Well, I've changed my mind," she said sadly. I knew then she was seeing and experiencing things that were breaking her heart, things that would one day break mine and change both of our lives forever.

In her province, Elizabeth was one of the rare few Westerners to be invited into what the Chinese call The Observation Room. We don't call them that here. We call them The Dying Rooms. Whenever I ask my audiences around the country if anyone has heard of The Dying Rooms, few people ever raise their hands. Oprah Winfrey did an hour long special on them a few years ago and probably shed more light on them than anyone ever has, yet hardly anyone in the Western world knows what they are.

The Dying Rooms are where abandoned babies are housed, after they are found and prior to an orphanage placement. And, because of the huge orphan problem, babies are found often - at shopping malls, bus terminals, police stations, etc. (As you know, my son Simon was left in a woods, and my daughter Danielle was abandoned at a hotel when she was around three or four years old.) When found, these children are sent to this nightmare, where survival of the fittest reigns supreme until an opening allows the next one to be moved to the local orphanage.

It is here where Elizabeth observed rows and rows of about fifteen wooden boxes. These served as makeshift cribs containing anywhere from one to three babies each. There were two "caretakers" to work the entire room. I use this term lightly as they didn't really provide care. They didn't pick up the children. Didn't hold them. Didn't comfort them or love on them in any way, in place of a mommy or daddy. At meal time, the workers would give each baby a bottle, crudely propped up against a rolled up towel. If the child was strong and had good control, they were able to feed themselves. If, however, they struggled with weakness, milk would run down their neck and chest causing rashes. Worse, sometimes the bottle would be fumbled away altogether, and with no assistance from the "caregivers", the little one would go hungry. On three occasions, Elizabeth witnessed dead babies being put into garbage bags and hauled out like they were trash.

Sometimes a child would die and be left in the box with a live baby for an extended period of time, until one of the staff ladies eventually entered the room and noticed. One horrific story involved a young mentally challenged man who worked at this place. Also an orphan, he was assigned the task of putting the dead children into the garbage bags. Perhaps he was the only one willing or compliant enough. One day, an older child about five years old was sent to the observation room. He had ingested some poisonous chemicals. His parents brought him to a hospital but when they realized he was terminal, they left him there. When the hospital discovered there was no one around to pay for his care, they sent him over to the Observation Room so he wouldn't be in the way. Can you imagine being a five-year-old in your last remaining moments of life? Can you even comprehend your parents, the adults you are closest to and trust more than anyone else on the planet, leaving you when you need them the most? Or how about a hospital unwilling to even attempt to save your life or to bring you comfort in your final moments because no one you know had a credit card handy?

So here he was now, in the same room as Elizabeth. She went to him for seven days in a row. That is how long he held on with no loved ones in sight. She would stroke his head, sing to him and pray for him. When he finally passed, the young man in charge of bagging the bodies came. Because this boy was larger than the infants, he awkwardly struggled in his duty. He had to use two garbage bags and at one point, Elizabeth was mortified as the young body flopped out onto the floor. She got up, went over to the worker and helped him place the boy properly into the bags and watched as he was carried off to another room to be incinerated.

Like I said, Elizabeth is the strongest woman I have ever met.

James

Elizabeth knew she had to do whatever it would take to save a child from that horrible place. She came home on a mission. Once we knew our relationship was heading in the right direction towards marriage, she informed me of two requirements for any man she was going to marry. The first one was that he had to be willing to adopt someday. Well, adoption had been a huge part of my family growing up, so no problem there. I always thought I would anyway. The second requirement was that the man she was going to marry had to be intensely good looking! OK, so one out of two ain't bad. (I told that joke while I was performing in Atlanta once, and a lady yelled out, "Who'd she marry?")

She also had the idea that she wanted our first child to be adopted. This could be a wonderful message to not only our first, but also to any subsequent, naturally birthed kids.

Adoption does not have to be an afterthought or a plan B. I was on board from the get go. One problem was, according to Chinese law, both parents have to be thirty years old. When we married, Elizabeth was only twenty-seven. We had to wait. With her Type A personality, my wife had all of the paperwork filled out and ready to go way before her thirtieth birthday. She even found out that although both of us had to be thirty, she could actually submit the paperwork when she was twenty-nine and a half years old. She had that day marked on the calendar. Besides kindergartners, how many full grown adults do you know who celebrate half birthdays?

After her trip to the orphanages, our Would You Rather game had been replaced by dreams and discussions of our future family as we hung out in the same park as before. I always wanted to adopt a child who had Down syndrome and we would joke that perhaps we could adopt a child from China with Down syndrome.

This truly was a joke, as children with such a degree of special needs were not placed on the waiting child list at that time. China was a very prideful nation, and didn't want the rest of the world to know they had "imperfect kids". In fact, most of the orphans listed as having "special needs" were no more extensive than cleft palates or birth marks. Greater physical or mental challenges were simply not considered as possible adoptable children. The general attitude of the government officials was that nobody in their right mind would want these children.

So we settled on the idea we would adopt an orphan from China, listed as having special needs but most likely with a very mild condition. A child with Down syndrome from the states would possibly come later. And again, with Elizabeth's Type A personality, she had done the research and chosen the perfect adoption agency for us. All of the wheels were turning as soon she had turned the infamous twenty-nine and a half, and off we went. After her first trip to China, Elizabeth had faithfully saved her money so we could pay a good portion of the costs of the adoption without scrambling. What a wise and frugal woman I married!

Many people don't realize the costs involved in a foreign adoption. The cost for an adoption from China, when all was said and done, was in the twenty-four thousand dollar range. There are home studies, background checks, filing fees, and fees by both the Chinese and U.S. governments. Additionally, once you are matched with a child and ready to go, there are plane tickets, hotel costs, food costs, drivers, and translators, all needed to bring your baby home.

This is where our story began to become comically God. Years earlier (before we were married and, ironically, while Elizabeth was in China on her first life changing trip), I had brought some teens from a church where I had been working to a Steven Curtis Chapman concert. Chapman is a well-known Grammy-winning Christian singer and songwriter. He and his wife Mary Beth are also adoptive parents to three children from China. While at his concert, I had wandered out to the hallway to explore some of his band merchandise and stop into the restroom. Walking along the hallway at Roberts Wesleyan College, near Rochester, N.Y., I came upon a display advertising a contest to win a guitar signed by Steven Curtis Chapman. I grabbed a pen and filled out a little card and shoved it into a cardboard box.

Within a few weeks, I realized that by filling out that card I had put myself onto the e-mail list for Shaohanna's Hope, an adoption ministry started by Steven Curtis and Mary Beth Chapman (now called Show Hope). I started receiving their e-newsletter on a regular basis. I never really paid much attention to the newsletter, giving it only a casual glance. The information provided was not really pertinent to where I was at during that particular moment in my life. At least, it wasn't until after I got married.

After we had begun the process of adoption, and after paying thousands of dollars in non-refundable deposits, I was getting ready to leave on tour with the band. I went to my office to grab some things and send out some e-mails. Back then I didn't have a laptop to bring with me on the road, so checking and sending e-mails was sporadic. I tried to get as much done as possible before leaving town. For some reason, I quickly glanced at the e-newsletter from Shaohanna's hope. There was a picture of a little boy called James with a caption that read something like "Urgent need of a family for this little boy from China with Down syndrome"! My interest was piqued. I scrolled down. An article went on to say that if a family didn't step up to adopt James, he would be put back into the system and may never be allowed out.

I called Elizabeth at work. Here is our conversation as best as I can remember it:

"Honey, I'm on the Shaohanna's Hope e-mail list and they are trying to find a couple to adopt a little boy from China who has Down syndrome." I explained the article.

"Wow! From China, uh? You're not saying we should adopt him are you?" she replied.

"I don't know, I'm just saying…" I said.

"We've already started the process with another agency. We've paid thousands of dollars. We can't just switch like that."

"OK. OK. I'm not saying we should. I just thought it was interesting that's all."

"Well, we can't adopt him, but why don't you call the number and see how we can be praying for him. By the way, I think you're the sexiest man alive."

"Thanks. I know it, but it's always nice to hear."

(So the last two sentences may not have happened exactly like that, but the rest is pretty accurate.)

Elizabeth later told me that when she hung up the phone, she affectionately laughed about me to her coworkers. She thought I was being ridiculous for having my heart strings plucked like that. After all, we had a plan.

I picked up the phone and called Shaohanna's Hope. My first question to the woman on the other end of the line was, "Did you have much response?" She explained that yes, they had received nearly 300 inquiries. Wow! Great! We were off the hook. James would be fine, we could stick to our plan and Elizabeth wouldn't have to mock me to her co-workers anymore. After a nice conversation about who I was and about my wife, the woman took down my contact info, just in case she had more to share later on for prayer requests.

Off on tour I went. Once in a while, in the quiet between concerts, when I could be alone in my thoughts on our RV headed to another city to perform, that little picture of that little boy with Ds would pop into my mind and I would say a prayer for him. Other than that, I pretty much put the matter behind me.

The very week I returned home, I was at my office once again catching up on e-mails. One had just come through from Shaohanna's Hope. It was a short, personal note which said something like, "Dan, would you and your wife re-consider adopting James. The family we thought we had fell through."

Hmm. Time to call my wife at work again. The conversation went something this:

"Hi, honey. Sorry to bother you at work, but I just received this e-mail from that lady at Shaohanna's hope." I read it to her.

"What are you saying? Do you think we should adopt him? Now we are even further down the road with our adoption agency. You can't just switch like that," she said.

"I know, I know. I'm just reading what this lady wrote to me," I replied.

"You said they had nearly 300 inquiries right? So he'll be fine. But why don't you call her again and see how we can be praying for him."

"Good idea. I'll call"

"By the way, I'm the luckiest woman alive. You had me at hello. You're the living embodiment of Brad Pitt and Matthew McConaughey combined."

"Thanks honey. That's a little overboard. But I appreciate it none the less."

(Yea, I know - a little far-fetched on the last two there.)

I picked up the phone. "Does this mean you have 299 other couples waiting in the wings to adopt James?" I asked the Shaohanna's Hope lady.

"No," she said. "Actually, most of those couples fell through and we think that only you and one other couple qualify."

Oh boy.

I may not be the smartest man in the world, but it did seem as though God was trying to get our attention. When I called Elizabeth, she could see Him waving His arms at us, too.

Elizabeth is a planner. She likes to do her research and have all of her ducks in a row. She suggested that we get together with my parents and discuss the possibility of us adopting a child with Down syndrome as our first child. She had always imagined us adopting a child with Ds later on after we had a few other children so she could get used to being a mom. This was definitely not part of her plan.

So after much prayer and discussion, research and thinking, Elizabeth felt as though we should not adopt little James. She asked if I was OK with that. I was fine and told her that we both had to be on board. We were concerned with the financial hit we would take having already paid so much money to a different adoption agency and, to be honest, I was so frightened with the prospect of being a dad that any delay in the inevitable helped to put me at ease. I did suggest that she call the woman at Shaohanna's Hope and let her know. That way if there were other issues or questions that had come up, nothing would be missed. I'm not too good at gathering the proper data to report back to my wife.

So, on a late Friday afternoon, Elizabeth called Shaohanna's Hope and told them we were not going to be the ones to adopt James. She later told me that even as the words were coming out of her mouth, she knew we were wrong. When she hung up the phone she was sobbing. It was a long weekend as she wrestled with what we had just done. We prayed even more and she asked me if I thought we should call back. Again, I told her that would be fine by me, but that we better be sure. We prayed together and separately.

Monday morning, my wife picked up the phone and called Shaohanna's Hope. Her words were something like, "You are probably going to think I'm a crazy woman, but we have changed our minds." That was the moment we realized God's plan was more important than ours. Who would have figured?

Howie

Our realization that this was totally a God thing was confirmed when Elizabeth told the adoption agency that we would be dropping them in order to work with the agency handling James. They were a wonderful, Christian organization who saw the value in what we were doing and quickly decided to refund almost all of our non-refundable deposits! This agency had never heard of another child with Down syndrome being adopted out of China to the U.S. and had never done this before, but they also knew God was doing something wonderful here.

At one point, the lady from Shaohanna's Hope told my wife that she knew of at least two people who were very excited that James was going to be adopted. She informed us that Mary Beth and Steven Curtis Chapman had been praying for him ever since they met him several months earlier at Hope Foster Home in China. In fact, they had been instrumental in getting him on the waiting child list. Wow! The biggest Christian singer/songwriter on the planet knew our soon-to-be son, James, personally! One little thing we were told though was that, for whatever reason, they called him Howie. Uh…OK.

Excitement consumed us as we prepped and planned for a new little one to arrive into our home. For the first time ever, I experienced my wife partaking in the ancient ritual of "nesting". Or as I like to call it, "Get the hell out of my way while I clean our house" syndrome. And I don't just mean clean. Our house was already pretty tidy. I mean deep, deep, cleaning. My wife became almost insane with the task of making a home for little Howie. I had never experienced this type of obsession before. I was a little afraid to come home, as I wasn't sure what project she would need my help with. Some tasks I like. Mowing - fine. Laundry - no problem. But others I hate - mopping, scrubbing, dusting and painting are beyond tedious for me. Elizabeth was on a mission more pressing than any 007 adventure, though. She was out for vengeance against any trace of dirt in our home.

I'm not sure about other adoptive fathers, but I can honestly say that my emotional experience during all of this was quite different from my wife's. From thousands of miles away Elizabeth was deeply in love with and bonded to Howie before ever having met him face to face. I was slightly disconnected. I kept asking myself when I would "feel" something for our waiting son and sometimes wondered if there was something wrong with me. When I saw pictures of Howie I thought he looked cute and all, but I wasn't longing after him in the same manner as Elizabeth. Part of me pondered when my emotions would kick in and I would experience this bonding to him like she had.

This adoption, for me, was partly an intellectual exercise. I knew we were doing a good thing. I knew that God had led us down this path and there was nothing wrong with our decision. But I worried just a little that I wouldn't be excited about being a dad. In fact, I was very nervous about the prospect. Sometimes, when even the slightest road bump in the process occurred, I would be secretly relieved. My fears ranged from being a crappy father to having certain aspects of my life disrupted once a child entered my world - like touring with the band or going out with friends.

Although we had some time to wait before we could travel overseas and bring Howie home, we found some reassurance in the fact that he was in a wonderful place called the Hope Foster Home. Prior to arriving at Hope, the people who received him from the police didn't notice his imperforate anus, an internal abnormality in which the intestines doesn't connect to an exit. So they fed him for a few days while he got fussier and fussier, each caregiver overlooking his lack of any bowel movements. Finally, a British doctor discovered his condition and acted quickly so he could receive surgery immediately - saving his life a second time in less than a week. Shortly after, Howie ended up at Hope, which was run by Dr. Joyce and her husband, Robin. Divine intervention kept him from being put into a state run orphanage, or even worse, the Dying Rooms.

Howie was about two years old when we were matched with him. My wife was in touch with Joyce and Robin and they sent us an occasional photo and updates on how he was doing. We were grateful for their loving care towards our little one and for their consistent communications and updates, and took comfort in the fact that he was at Hope, instead of at a not-so-nice place like the one Elizabeth had experienced first-hand. Until...

The news hit us like a punch in the gut. Howie had been moved. Apparently there was a political conflict in the province where he was found. Not sure of the details, and it really didn't matter. All we knew is that Howie was removed and brought to an orphanage in Langfang. Elizabeth was especially distraught. She had seen the conditions of some of the places where he was headed. We knew nothing of his new destination, but the not knowing made things even worse. It was a tough few months. Our church family prayed with us often. We just wanted our young boy to be safe, well-fed and taken care of. Now, it was a black hole of silence. Day after day dragged by as we worried that little Howie was not in an ideal atmosphere. Until…

If there was any hint of doubt in my mind of the sincerity and genuine kindness of Steven Curtis Chapman and his wife Mary Beth, it would have all ended during this devastating period for us. Over time, admittedly, I had become a bit cynical about the music industry. Especially the Christian music industry. My band The Dig Project and I had the privilege of being able to record, tour and perform for thousands of mostly young people. We loved what we did and enjoyed all of the blessings which came with being a touring rock band. However, to the Christian music industry, we were outsiders. Even after signing with a small indie label, we often felt like the red-headed step child of their roster. We had experienced others with massive egos. We heard and saw things that should have no part of anything with Christ's name attached to it. So, although I had an inclination that Steven Curtis was the real deal, now I could be sure.

At one point during a trip to the Hope Foster Home in China, Steven and Mary Beth took a great deal of extra effort to seek out and find Howie's new home in an orphanage about an hour and a half outside of Beijing. Suddenly, by e-mail, we received a little ray of light. Two short video clips, about 11 seconds and 15 seconds showing that our soon to be son was OK. Mary Beth was holding him and he was safe! This wasn't much, but it did relieve some of the strain of not knowing. The silence had been broken!

This was not something the Chapman's had to do. They could have taken their trips to China and back home having never made this incredible gesture. They went the extra mile (several miles actually) to bring a small measure of peace to a worried couple shrouded in unnerving anticipation. Yup. The real deal. They are a couple who live out a sincere and genuine faith in Christ. I am less cynical now about those in the Christian music industry. It seems, perhaps, that God has blessed the Chapmans for a reason.

8

Simon

My wife once asked me, "Honey, if by some chance we get matched with a little boy when we adopt, would it be OK if we named him Simon?" When she was working in an orphanage in China, she had become particularly close to a little boy with the same name. Once she was home, though, he had passed away (a few weeks before our son was born), and it was her desire to remember this child by naming one of her own Simon. I agreed, although I had it mind that my first son would be named Wyatt Earp Kulp. Oh well, a novelty name definitely does not win over something as emotionally stirring as the request Elizabeth had made. So, while this young orphan from China was known to some as James and yet to others as Howie, for us, he was Simon.

Finally after much waiting and uncertainty, we were given the green light. It was time to go! Elizabeth's dream of the past few years was about to come true. Once again, Simon was her son and she was his mom and she felt this deeply, way down in her soul. I was still not feeling that sort of connection yet, but I was excited nonetheless. I had never been out of the country before, with the exception of Canada, and that doesn't really count as far as I'm concerned. After all, we're talking an entirely different culture, language and money. So, while a big part of me was excited, I was also a bit nervous. However, knowing that Elizabeth had gone twice before was a comfort, and eased any stress I might have had.

We finally landed in Beijing after about a 22 hour plane ride. With very little effort, we found our guide, along with several other couples who also were there to adopt. We were all ushered onto a bus and whisked off to a hotel. My eyes were wide as I looked around at all of the huge buildings. Everything about this place was different – from the architecture to even the odors. I wanted to soak it all up, believing that this was a once in a lifetime trip. My thoughts were soon interrupted by our Chinese contact from the adoption agency. "Mr. and Mrs. Kulp?" she asked as she leaned over the seats. "We want you to know that we have made every arrangement in case you change your mind."

Change our mind? That was an odd statement. And also not one extended to the other adoptive couples on the bus. We played dumb even though we knew where she was headed. "What do you mean?" we asked.

"We have made every arrangement in case you change your mind and decide you don't want him". She went on to explain (and we thought this was funny), "You do know he has a little Down syndrome don't you?"

"Yes, we know. Don't worry, we won't change our minds"

"Well, you will have to be very patient with him."

"No problem."

"He will probably be delayed from other children his age."

My wife finally said, "Look, if he has eight arms and he's purple we will still want him."

As I stated previously, China is a very prideful nation and didn't want the rest of the world to know they had "imperfect" children. So they hid them. They put them away in institutions, in the same fashion my father had been urged to do with my brother Matthew. Everywhere we went in China, people were fairly incredulous that we would want this child with Down syndrome.

While many of the adoptive parents from our travel group had to wait a few days, we were headed to Simon's orphanage the very day after our arrival. Obviously Elizabeth had a hard time sleeping, as the air was filled with anticipation. After all, this was the fulfillment of all of her hopes and dreams for the last few years. I was still a bit nervous by the fact that I hadn't yet felt the same emotional attachment to our soon-to-be son that my wife had been experiencing for a very long time. What if upon meeting him, I was still detached?

The trip to the orphanage was about an hour away from our hotel. Our adoption agency had provided a driver and an interpreter named Akim. At first I was wary of these new helpers in our lives. I guess my imagination was a flurry of scenes from movies where the Americans were victimized or conned in some way by the natives of a foreign land. However, over the course of our trip, I would become very fond of Akim. He was in his early twenties and not only very smart, but very street savvy, too. As I looked at some of the other couples with their interpreters, I was very grateful for ours. He knew exactly how to help us navigate through the red tape of adoption as well as some of the cultural and relational aspects of life in China. He knew when to step forward and when to stay in the background. Most of all, he got my sense of humor. To this day, many years later, I still keep in touch with Akim and am grateful for his friendship. Thank you, Facebook!

Elizabeth was bubbling over with excitement. Each delay in our journey intensified the anticipation. At one point, our driver was a bit lost and had to pull over to ask for directions. I thought my wife was going to explode out of her skin. But before we knew it, we were headed down a back alley brimming with activity from street vendors and other assorted workers. We took a left hand turn and before us was a nondescript, run down building. This was it!

Upon entering, we were directed to a plain, shabby office. Akim exchanged dialogue with a head nanny and we were told to sit and wait for the director of the orphanage. We sat. More waiting.

The director finally entered. He was not what you would call a warm individual. He shook our hands and immediately went to his small desk. For about ten minutes, he spoke harshly into the phone with a raised voice and an annoyed look on his face. I had no idea what was going on but it didn't seem to faze Elizabeth all that much. I was becoming quite nervous. What if this one man decides he doesn't want us to have Simon? Or that things hadn't been done to his satisfaction. He sure looked belligerent and my imagination was running wild. Elizabeth later explained to me that this was sort of a cultural demeanor for the Chinese. To Western ears, they can look and sound very angry sometimes, even when they are not. Especially during business type settings.

Without warning, there he was! Simon was carried in by a worker. He was wearing a puffy pink winter coat. This was because the majority of orphans are girls, so it is girls clothing which gets passed around from child to child. When a child is adopted out, the only clothing they take with them is what they are wearing at the time. The rest is left for the ones left behind.

The glow on my wife's face was unmatched by anything I had ever seen on her face before. It was amazing to watch as this little boy was placed in my wife's arms for the very first time. I was in charge of holding the video camera and I made sure I captured every moment (knowing she would kill me if I failed in my task). (The link to this video can be found at the end of the book.)

Simon took it all in stride. He wore a look of wonderment and curiosity. Who were these new strangers who had just entered into his life? Yet he seemed very comfortable in his new mommy's arms too. The moment was magical.

Even more magical was that, shortly after getting back into the van, Simon fell asleep in Elizabeth's arms. Car seats are not used in China, but no matter, nothing could make him unsafe in her arms. Not after all she had been through to get him home. She looked at me with her beautiful big eyes and gave me a look and a sigh as if to say, "Finally." After all of her praying, hoping and dreaming. After mountains of paperwork and bureaucratic obstacle courses. After all of the hoops she had jumped through, she now held our son in her arms, and tears of joy began to flow while Simon slept in peace and security. He would never again be without a mom and a dad.

I was now a father, and it took longer than an actual pregnancy. I was excited that the wait was over. I was thrilled to be doing something positive in this world, as I can be a pretty selfish dude. I was still unsure about the whole emotional connection to my new son, but I was about to have the opportunity to put my apprehensions to the test.

After arriving back to our hotel room, the first thing Elizabeth did was to give Simon a bath. It seemed as if this was a luxury that had been missing from his life. His hair was like a scouring pad and his skin was leathery dry. Our suspicions were confirmed when we removed his clothes. It appeared to us that Simon loved being naked! It also occurred to us that this was probably a very rare experience for him too. He rubbed his tiny hands all over his body, especially up and down his arms. The real fun began when we placed him in the tub for the first time. It was as if we had just unleashed him into Willy Wonka's Chocolate Factory! He smiled and splashed and splashed and smiled. He didn't just splash either. His hands beat down upon the water in a magnificent fury while his legs kicked back and forth with reckless abandoned. Elizabeth and I laughed and watched with great joy as our son romped in the water like he probably never had, literally, before.

Elizabeth had to go to a meeting regarding some paperwork for the adoption. She would still be in the hotel, but for the first time, I would be alone with my new son. I had not done much in the way of child care before. Growing up, there were nine of us kids, but I was the second to youngest. I never even changed a diaper before. As a child, everyone did that for me. As an adult, I had taught a Vacation Bible School class a couple of years in a row but most of my kids were never younger than fifth graders. Most of my work experience was as a youth pastor, working with teenagers.

So I relied on what I did know about young ones. Play! We had brought a yellow and blue striped toy bee with us. Simon sat at the head of the hotel bed and I sat at the foot of it. I tossed it to him. He picked it up, tossed it back, and smiled while doing it. Not only was he having fun, but this little game also told me that he was a pretty sharp kid, too. Each time I tossed it, he would retrieve it and toss it back. If he didn't make it all the way to me at the other end of the bed, he was determined to try over, tossing it once again. We were having fun! My emotional thermometer was rising.

After a while, Simon seemed tired. So I sat in the lounger in our room and held him in my arms the way I had observed other parents doing. He stared up at me with his deep, brown eyes, and I sang to him the first song that popped into my head, "Amazing Grace." I never could have imagined the feelings associated with being a father. Man, I was hooked! Simon was my son, and I was his dad. I knew from this moment on that I would always look at him as what I felt he was - my own flesh and blood.

By week two, we were in Guangzhou. This is the final destination for every parent waiting to adopt a child. There are required medical exams, paperwork and a visit to the American Consulate to make your son or daughter an official citizen of your own country, complete with a swearing in ceremony. Guangzhou is a very nice city. All of us were put in a beautiful hotel called the White Swan. During the days we would walk the streets and visit little shops and eat authentic Chinese food. After a few days, Elizabeth began to make friends with one particular shop owner in a tiny store she frequented with Simon. On about the third or fourth day, Elizabeth could see the wheels turning in the shop owner's mind as she looked at Simon sitting in his stroller. Finally the woman mustered up the courage to ask flat out why we had a boy. Again, most Westerners adopted girls, unless the boys have very mild special needs. Elizabeth tried to explain Down syndrome to the woman but she did not understand. As Elizabeth looked up, she saw an English/Chinese dictionary up on the shelf. Reminiscent of my father looking up the word "Mongoloid" in a dictionary, she looked up the words "Down syndrome" and handed the book to the shop owner. Once she was finished reading, the woman looked up and said, "You are very foolish."

"Why?" Elizabeth responded.

"Because in our country, we have a test, and if we find out that the baby inside of us has that [Down syndrome], we get rid of it." She went on to express how foolish it would be to keep a son like Simon and added, "He's never going to be able to tell you he loves you."

Wow. What else can you say? If a human life is different from "the norm," just get rid of it. Come to think of it, though, this is not too different from what happens in our own country. Almost 90% of all women in America who have the test and find out their child "might" have Down syndrome also choose to abort. What a shame. How do you combat such ignorance?

You do exactly what my wife did in this situation and what my Mom and Dad did so many years earlier. You share the blessing of your children with special needs with others who need to have it. For the rest of our time in Guangzhou, Elizabeth intentionally wandered into that shop day after day with Simon in his stroller to say hi and let the shop owner see what a wonderful creation Simon truly is.

Elizabeth could have been offended. She could have stayed away. But what good would have been done? Like my mother, I believe the way to change the hearts and minds of people towards others is exposure. Indeed, people need to rub elbows with and experience the blessings that are the reality of anyone who raises, works with or is related to anyone with special needs.

I think some of the most annoying people are those without kids who claim that, although they don't have children, that they are, in fact, parents. Of course they are talking about their pets. Oh, shut up. There is no comparison. And, if you have both children and an animal, I would find it highly disturbing if you felt as strongly about your family pet as you did your own child. The only people whoever say something this dumb are the ones who are ga ga over their pet but have no children to compare it to. Trust me, the emotions of having a child are off the chart.

If I sound hard on these pet owners, let me admit to you this: I like cats. I have a cat. Before I had kids, every night my cat (Birdie - that's right, I said her name is Birdie) would climb up on my chest as my wife and I watched TV and would nuzzle her cute little nose on to my face. She would also give me kisses, getting as close to my lips as possible without actually touching them. Cute. Very cute. I even said this to Elizabeth once: "Honey, I can't imagine that children are going to be as cute and lovable as this cat. She's the best." My wife knew better and thought I was pretty dumb.

And guess what? I was! You know what happened after adopting my children? Our beloved Birdie has become like furniture. I mean, don't get me wrong, I still think she is a great pet. But that is all she is - a great pet. And, again, there really is no comparison of a great pet to your children. Trust me. And, please, if you are among one of the childless couples who might respond to a family with actual children with something like, "Oh, we have kids too. They're puppies" or "My wife and I don't have kids yet, but we have a pet ferret," understand this: you sound ridiculous. Sorry. You'll just have to give birth or adopt to know what I am talking about. (I'll give you a pass if your family pet is a chimpanzee. They are probably not only challenging to raise, but I could also see myself getting pretty darn emotionally attached.)

9

Danielle

Sometimes, I hear horror stories about tough adjustments for orphans who have been adopted. Who could blame them? First they are abandoned, and then they are ripped from the only world they have ever known. Even though the new world they are about to experience will most likely be leaps and bounds better than their current life, change is not easy for some.

People often ask how the adjustment was for Simon, and I can honestly answer that it was perfect. He immediately took to us and we immediately took to him. Jackpot! And, for about two years, he was the rock star of our family, receiving all of the attention that an only child would receive from a mom and dad. Life was good.

It was very good. But not necessarily complete yet for Elizabeth. She had begun exploring the web to check up on the orphan situation in China. Somehow, she was led to a little girl on the waiting child list named Danielle, who was about to turn seven. While we had been told that Simon might be the first child with Ds adopted out of China to the U.S., there had been a second one spoken for by another family. Danielle was the third. This was good news. It meant that China was beginning to become more comfortable with putting children with Ds on the list, realizing that there are couples who actually want these children!

You know when someone really wants something from you, then acts like they really don't by kidding about it? This was Elizabeth's tactic with me. She really wanted to adopt Danielle. I was not ready. So instead of nagging me or begging me, she simply joked about us adopting her. She joked a lot. Relentlessly. You know, like, "Hey honey, what would you like with the pizza I'm ordering for dinner tonight? How about another child from China?" Ha ha. Or she might ask, "Do you know what would go really nice in our living room? A daughter!" It became annoying because, as I said, I just wasn't ready.

I was still touring with the band. I was still not making much money doing it. I was still finding my footing with being a new dad. I had so many reasons to not adopt another child yet. I figured one day we would have more children. I just didn't figure it would be so soon.

One night at band rehearsal, I had a spiritual experience. Bill, our guitarist, was showing us some new songs. One particular riff brought an image to mind. I was remembering a story someone had told me about an orphanage they had gone to where a young boy with Cerebral Palsy was left in a chair all day and all night, in the same corner of the room, every day, to constantly stare at the same view. Even though he was cognitively typical, this is how the workers chose to treat him. This was his life. He would probably never know anything different. I began to sing the words "Bless the ones/Bless the ones who find them". Other lyrics came forth, and I found myself crying over these children and grateful for people like my wife who have been given an extra sensitivity to finding the ones who need to be found. My song was a prayer to God to bless men and woman like her. I didn't tell the guys what I was experiencing, but I went home and woke my wife up at about 1:00 am to tell her of my epiphany. I did not want Danielle's current life to be the only one she would ever know. "Are you serious?" she asked. "Seriously?" She leaped out of bed, bursting with excitement. "Now, I don't want you to be doing this just because I have been joking with you so much about it. I don't want you to think I was trying to pressure you." Yeah. Right.

I went to sleep. Mrs. Type A stayed up the rest of the night filling out the paperwork.

This time, the process seemed to go much faster. Once again, I was secretly grateful for any delay. Yes, God had impressed it on my heart that we needed to do this, but if He was also going to put up some road blocks here and there, this was fine by me. Not much luck; everything went very smoothly.

So we were headed back to China. This time, instead of having anxiety about going to a foreign country, I was actually looking forward to the return. I very much enjoyed the culture and the experiences and especially the food! This time too, Elizabeth brought her parents. Now, I didn't have to be the one to hold the video camera.

Different from our last trip, we would not be able to meet Danielle until a few days after our arrival. So we enjoyed the sights and enjoyed watching Elizabeth's parents, Steve and Kathy, take everything in for the first time. On the third day, Elizabeth had an adventure planned that I will talk about later. So we would break off from the group and allow her parents to go on and enjoy themselves without us.

Danielle was in a province quite a distance from Beijing and it required another plane trip. On the fifth day, we were driven to a government building with one other American adoptive family to meet Danielle and take her with us. It was disappointing not to see where she lived, but each province does things differently. This was an official looking building. As we entered, the other family was able to meet their new children almost immediately - a brother and a sister. We were told Danielle had not yet arrived. So we sat and waited. Eventually, I saw a young girl wander out into the lobby with no fanfare or announcement. Could this be her, I wondered? I elbowed Elizabeth. "Is that her?" She looked different from her pictures but it could very well have been her.

Elizabeth approached her and reached out her hand. At that moment we were both fairly certain. Danielle took her hand without fear, we looked around for validation. "Is this Danielle?" my wife asked. The interpreter, officials and orphanage workers came and verified that, indeed, this little girl was Danielle. She seemed content, curious and fairly mellow, all at the same time. We led her over to a play area and gave her a small backpack that my parents had bought for her. It was filled with goodies we anticipated she would enjoy. She unzipped the bag and went through each item and seemed thrilled to be receiving such gifts. Her speech was excitable and energetic and seemed to be a mix of real Chinese and gibberish. After signing some papers, we were headed back to the hotel.

That afternoon, once again, after giving her a bath, my wife was headed to a meeting to sign more papers, and I was left with my new daughter. She was hysterical as she went through all of the gifts and new clothes that Elizabeth had beautifully displayed for her. She especially seemed to enjoy the coloring books and would take them out and very loudly read from them with her own hybrid language. She made me laugh and at one point on some video I shot while my wife was gone, you can joyfully hear me exclaim, "I think we won the jackpot again, honey!"

For that entire day, once again, everything was perfect. We foresaw another wonderful transition for our new daughter. Until the next day...

Danielle started having some difficult emotional outbursts which would last for long periods of time. She would break down sobbing and would even lash out with what seemed like rage. Kicking, pinching and hitting, she would cry out, seeming without a trigger. Our heads were spinning and confused as to what seemed to be the problem.

Our best guess is this: I believe the orphanage neglected to tell us they were medicating her to keep her behaviors under wraps. For them, they probably took the easiest course of action to deal with her behavioral challenges. When we first met her, she did seem to be rather sedated. As I said, mellow. I imagine that once we had her, and she was no longer taking whatever it was they medicated her with, she was going through some pretty heavy withdrawals. Add to this the tremendous life changes this little girl had experienced in the last forty eight hours, and you can see how anyone's world would have been rocked.

Suddenly our perfect trip to get our second perfect child had become far more challenging. We never knew when she would have another episode and this kept us on pins and needles. It was especially tough in public places because her society was simply not accepting of those with special needs. We were not only stared at the way we had been during our trip to get Simon, but we were looked at with disdain. And so was our daughter. These stares once again weighed on us. We so wanted someone to give us a reassuring smile, or meet us with warm eyes. For the most part, this would not come until we were back in the states.

I was quickly burning out and Elizabeth was the trouper here. Running through my head over and over was the fear that we had made a big mistake. I hated this feeling, but it loomed over me. I was so incredibly close to Simon. Much to my wife's chagrin, he had ended up being a Daddy's boy. I missed him terribly and our new situation only made me long to be with him even more.

The plane ride home was especially rough. Even as helpful as Steve and Kathy had been for the entire trip, we were still overwhelmed by a force with which we were completely unfamiliar. Frankly, these behaviors were not like traits I had seen in others with Down syndrome. Often, we had to physically restrain Danielle for long periods of the twenty-two hour plane trip home. My wife took most of the shifts, I think partly out of a motherly instinct for her daughter and partly out of watching her husband's resolve crumble before her eyes. By the time we had landed in the U.S., my wife had several bruises, scratches and a bloody lip. Amidst my selfishness and self-pity, even I could see the parallels between what she had endured for the love of her daughter and what Jesus had done for the love of us. A verse kept popping into my head from the book of Isaiah: "He was wounded for our transgressions; He was bruised for our iniquities" (NKJV). Once again, I was in awe of this woman, the strongest woman I had ever met.

The next several weeks were equally challenging. Danielle would wake up several times each night. Sometimes crying. Sometimes hyper. Sometimes getting into things. And often, still having moments of emotional outbursts. At one point, in what I think was my darkest hour of fatherhood, I said to my mother-in-law Kathy, "Someone has to help us. You need to help us figure this out. Because she is ruining our lives!"

A few days later, my father came over to the house and sat with me to talk for a while. I figured he had heard about my struggles. He shared with me his own struggles he had had with one of his own adopted children. How he had regretted some of his own reactions. Although he didn't have advice for me, just the fact that he came to spend time with me, and me knowing he knew what I was going through, had meant the world to me. I was so grateful for his visit.

I am ashamed by my reactions to Danielle and for the worry I caused my wife. Elizabeth was afraid I wasn't going to bond with Danielle. I probably was causing as much turmoil in our home at this time as Danielle was. Although I paint a bleak picture, it wasn't all negative. Even I could see some wonderful traits about Danielle. She was vibrant and full of life. Funny, too. She loved to laugh and make others laugh. Her smile melted my heart. She adored her new younger brother. She was also quite a helper. There were many moments woven in and out of these first few months which I should have been able to hang my hat on. I think my biggest flaw was having not stepped back and looked at the big picture. Being short sighted.

Somehow, I forgot that the God I serve changes things. He makes all things new. He is never done working on people.

He wasn't finished with Danielle, but He wasn't done with me yet, either. As time went on, we began to get a handle on Danielle's behaviors. She would also begin to settle in to her new world, too. Finally, after getting through all of this, and despite the fact that, unlike her brother, Danielle is a Mama's girl, I can safely say that I am as bonded to her as my daughter as I am with my son Simon. I only wish I had been a stronger man during the rough times and not so short sighted. But hey, that's what my wife was for, right?

10

Searching for Simon's Past

As I said in the previous chapter, a few days into our second trip to China to adopt Danielle, my wife had an adventure planned. She hoped to track down the person who found Simon, abandoned in the woods, just a few hours after his birth. She wanted to get a clearer picture of the history of our little miracle boy, and thank the person who saved his life.

At first I was unenthused. I thought it would be like searching for a needle in haystack. I told her, "Honey, I don't know if you've noticed, but there are a lot of people here!" It seemed to me to be a futile endeavor that prevented us from joining her parents on some cool sight-seeing destinations.

However, as often is the case, my wife's enthusiasm was contagious. She hired a driver and a college student we met at our hotel to be our interpreter. I would be the videographer to document our adventure, and my excitement grew as the day progressed.

The only information we had about that fateful day when our son was discovered was a one page police report written in Chinese. Our first stop would be the police station in the same village where the woods were located, about two hours north of Beijing. Our driver looked over the report and headed in that direction.

The stop was very brief and the police were cooperative. They told us the location of the nearby woods, and also the identity of the man who found Simon. His name was Mr. Han and, according to the police report, he lived in the next town over from the woods.

Soon, we were standing amidst tall, straight trees perfectly aligned in row upon row. We were unsure of exactly where Simon had been placed. We walked around for several minutes and imagined the awful scenario of that day as we stared at different trees, patches of grass and shrubbery. Was he left out in the open? Was he well hidden? Did he have a blanket? Did his mother drop him off here? Father or family member? Did they live nearby? Questions were racing through our minds.

I videotaped our search in the woods. At one point on the video, you can hear me making a joke to lighten our mood, but as I turned around and faced my wife she was sobbing. As I often do, I felt like a jerk. I was attempting to add levity to a very somber moment. This was, in fact, the place where my son could have perished four years earlier. We took pictures and shot some more video. This was seemingly a profound moment, but ultimately, we saw a more complete picture of Simon's past. As if we now knew him more deeply.

Continuing on our journey, we went to the next village. All we had was a name: Mr. Han. Shortly after crossing into the next town, we noticed an elderly man walking along side of the dirt road. This was the very first person we saw and it was a long shot, but our driver pulled his car over and hopped out. He spoke with the older man for a couple of minutes.

The driver waved us out of the car. This man knew Mr. Han! His name was Mr. Wong and he told us to follow him. We headed down muddy paths and passed beside very small and run down, hut-like homes. After about a five minute hike, apparently we had arrived. This kindly and jovial old man pointed to a home and proceeded to just walk right in. He beckoned us to follow. Although brimming with excitement, we were a bit wary of just barging into someone else's house. But the smiling stranger continued to wave to us to follow him inside.

Upon entering this very modest one room house, we were introduced to a young girl, about twelve years old, sitting on what appeared to be a sleeping mat for the whole family. She was blowing up balloons and placing them into a basket. We soon found that this was Mr. Han's granddaughter. Our college student interpreter explained to the little girl why these Americans were now invading her home. She became excited and said she would run into town to find her grandparents, who were now working their day jobs. In a matter of minutes, we would be meeting the hero who saved our son!

As I sat there taking in my surroundings, I was grateful that we had arrived here with relative ease and was appreciative of my wife's can-do spirit of adventure. The simplicity of this house also struck me. These folks did not have the amenities that we enjoy in the U.S. The floor was a sort of hardened dirt. There was a TV in the corner showing a fuzzy episode of Tom and Jerry. But none of the comforts and excesses typical of an American home. It was evident this family probably had very little. So, now, I was thankful for all I had been given in life and was available to me.

Our gregarious host, who led us here, laughed and spoke loudly in Chinese to our interpreter. I didn't know what he was saying unless it was translated for me, but I sure got a kick out of Mr. Wong's larger than life personality. He, too, seemed delighted to be involved in a unique and unfolding story.

Within minutes, the granddaughter returned to the house with an older woman. She was the grandmother, a smiling, heavy set woman who never once seemed to flinch at the idea that three strangers, two of them white Americans, were occupying her living room/bedroom/dining area. Our interpreter began to explain why we were there and told the story of Simon. Mrs. Han explained to us that she was also present when her husband found our baby laying in the forest! While I held the video camera, Elizabeth excitedly began to ask questions.

The Hans, along with others from their village, had been hired to clear a forest of any debris, like garbage and fallen branches, so that it would be more pristine come springtime. As Mr. and Mrs. Han were combing the woods, they came across Simon laying on the ground, wrapped in a sheet. This day was December 28th, 2004. There was snow on the ground and it had, in fact, been snowing when they found him! The Chinese couple picked him up and carried him to a nearby shed. They spent the next several hours warming him up and keeping him safe. Eventually they called the police, who came and filled out a report and took the newborn from them.

Elizabeth had brought along a photo album of Simon, with various pictures of his time with us. We were able to explain how well he was doing, that because of their simple act of kindness, a valuable and worthy life was allowed to live on, and make an American couple very happy. Mrs. Han seemed pleased.

Finally, Mr. Han entered the house. He was an impressive man. Strong features and classically Chinese. He looked like he should be in the movies. Once again, our presence was explained to him. He seemed very excited to have us there and looked at the photos of Simon with pleasure.

I was struck by their hospitality, too. One of my hesitations when Elizabeth first told me of her idea for this quest was, "What if these people don't want to be found? Maybe they just want to be left alone?" But now, here we were, from the other side of the world, and they kept offering us water. One thing we knew about international travel was to never drink their water! We had brought our own and politely declined. We hoped we weren't offending them. Next thing we knew, Mr. Han was handing some money to his granddaughter so she could run into town and buy meat to feed his guests. Our interpreter filled us in. Again, we politely declined and hoped we weren't offending them in any way. What a wonderful family. Having almost nothing, the first thing on their mind was to try and feed us a dinner.

They also granted us the privilege of taking pictures with them so that we could remember this part of Simon's story, too. I requested a picture of just me with Mr. Han. I told him I wanted a picture of me shaking the hand of the man who saved my son's life. He graciously obliged. It is among one of my favorites.

Thank you Elizabeth, for such a wonderful and unforgettable day!

The X-Man

A couple months after arriving home with Danielle, the doctor's asked if we would like to have a routine genetic test done on her. Part of me thought, "Why bother? We already know she has Down syndrome". But we went ahead with it, feeling that it couldn't hurt. We did notice she had some features uncharacteristic of someone with that extra chromosome. For one, she was tall and lanky for her age. Her fingers looked like those of a concert pianist and she had large feet. My wife had noticed in China that Danielle's lifeline on her hand was the same as a typical person's. Despite wondering about these traits, we just wrote it off as something unique to her. After all, the Chinese government couldn't possibly have misdiagnosed her.

A couple of weeks later we were called in to the geneticists' office at Strong Memorial Hospital in Rochester, N.Y. The doctor looked at us and said, "Your daughter does not have Down syndrome." We were stunned; my wife started to cry. For her, this was an emotional issue simply because now she was mourning the loss of something she thought she had. My wife is probably one of the only women in the world who cried when she found out her child did NOT HAVE DOWN SYNDROME!

There is a famous poem in the Down syndrome community of parents. It is called "Welcome to Holland" and was written by a parent who describes receiving the news that her newborn baby had Ds. She said it was like going on a journey in which the plane she was traveling did not land in the expected destination, but instead in Holland. She talks about how although it wasn't the planned place to go, it had a joy and beauty all of its own.

Well, we felt like we had landed on a runway in Holland only to suddenly have the plane take off again before we even got out. Destination unknown!

The doctor went on to explain that Danielle had something called Alfi's syndrome. She said it was a genetic mutation where part of her ninth chromosome was missing. She also said that there was a little genetic material on the end of her ninth chromosome which needed further analysis, and if that extra material ended up being from her 21st Chromosome, it would be sort of like she had…wait for it…wait for it…A LITTLE DOWN SYNDROME! (See chapter 8)

Did I mention that my wife is Type A personality? This new diagnosis was more unsettling for her than for me. The doctor kept talking about a genetic mutation and I thought, "Cool! My daughter is an X-Man! She is going to hit puberty and develop the gift of invisibility." For Elizabeth, however, this was uncharted territory. She had studied Down syndrome. She knew Down syndrome. But Alfi's syndrome was not on our radar; we had never even heard of it before. As we sat there listening to the sounds of the airplane taking off from Holland, I knew Elizabeth would feel a bit more on top of the situation as soon as she had the chance to read up on everything she could find on Alfi's syndrome (the official name, by the way, is 9p-).

Together we learned (and when I say together, I mean she did all of the research and then told me what she found) that Alfi's syndrome is very rare and that there only about 125 reported cases in the whole U.S. and about 250 in the whole world. (Since our original research, these numbers have increased a bit, possibly due to more accurate diagnoses). Because of the rarity of this condition, the data is very limited. What we do know is that people with this diagnosis tend to have hyperactivity coupled with pronounced mood swings and emotional outbursts. They can also be very social, compassionate, empathetic, funny, lively and have cheery dispositions. On a physical level, they seem to have issues with kidneys and ovaries. Their skulls tended to fuse together, sometimes requiring surgery to create more space. And Danielle, like her brother, would be mentally delayed and in need of Special Education.

Despite a new set of challenges, once again we were reminded of the power and sovereignty of God. You see, if the Nation of China had known that Danielle did not have Down syndrome, they may have never let her out of the country. Because of families coming forward to adopt children with Ds, proving they were really wanted, it seemed as if they were becoming slightly more comfortable with these children being placed on the waiting child list. I have the feeling they would have hidden Danielle away forever in an orphanage. I believe God guided them to diagnose her wrongly in order to get her out. For me, this all boils down to this: Score! Kulp's 2, China 0.

I think because of my upbringing, after we adopted Simon, I was proud and a little arrogant that my household had an extra chromosome. In my mind, I mocked other families missing this trait with a childlike taunt – "na na nana na, our house has an extra chromosome!" But, then, we adopted Danielle and she evened us right back out.

12

I'm a Jerk

Since high school, I have been involved with many ministries, from church youth work to parachurch organizations, the lead singer of a touring Christian rock band to a writer for a Christian web site, just to name a few. I have led teens on domestic mission trips and volunteered my "time, treasures and talents" in order to serve both the Body of Christ and the unchurched world. I gave my best efforts and had become well-versed in the Christian subculture, and had the privilege of hearing some of our nations' greatest Christian teachers, preachers, pastors and theologians. My parents left me with a wonderful legacy and an awesome example to follow. On paper, it looked as if I had it all together as a fan of Jesus and a pillar of compassion.

The little secret I held in my heart and in my head told a different story though. Despite having been immersed in the message of love and grace found in the Bible, and having received every advantage to learn and understand this very basic tenet of the Christian faith, the truth is, that I am a jerk.

At one of my last shows before heading off to Eastern Europe, a friend came up to me after the event and said, "You've got a great job. You get to brag about your kids for two hours at each performance!" He's right. And, because this is true, people often approach me and say something like, "You and your wife are amazing!" or offer a similar sentiment.

I want to clear this fallacy up right now. My wife is amazing. I am not. I'm a jerk. It's true. While Elizabeth really is an amazing woman, wife and mother, I simply receive the benefits of her being a class act. I think sometimes people listen to my story and think I am some sort of Super Dad. Well, the truth will set you free right? So, here it is. Enjoy your freedom.

I'm forty-one years old and pretty set in my ways. I like things the way I like them. If I put something somewhere, I don't want it to be moved. If my CD player is on a certain volume, that is where I want it to stay. I like my DVD's in cases (the case that matches the corresponding disc would be nice, too) and don't like when I find them separated. I crave peace in my home and hate, absolutely hate, interruptions. How do these desires play out in a home with two (about to be three) children with special needs, you ask? They don't. As a result, I'm prone to irritability. I'm moody. I get grumpy when I'm tired. A far cry from Ward Clever.

Elizabeth laughs at me because I don't like change, and yet we are an ever-changing family. Super Dad I certainly am not. Sure, I have my strong points, but again, more often than I would like to admit, instead of Pa Ingalls, my kids got stuck with an exasperated father who lacks the stamina to keep up and the patience to enjoy trying.

I'm that guy. You know, the jerk. When I'm in the express lane at the grocery store, I count the amount of groceries in the cart of the person in front of me. One item over the 20 or less statute, and I'm sighing heavily, rolling my eyes or thinking bad thoughts. Crappy service, rude managers or line budgers are all in the crosshairs for my crankiness, too, as far as I'm concerned. I'm the best driver on the road and most others drive like idiots. In short, most of the time I live my life under the assumption that everyone should think like me and act accordingly. Seldom seems to happen, though.

So, what is a Christian man like me supposed to do? The very title of "Christian" means "Christ-like", or "little Christ". Not only do I fall way short in the father and husband role, I pretty much blow it in the most important pursuit one can commit to. Being transformed into the likeness of my Friend and Savior.

My jerkiness extends far back. I can remember years ago when Elizabeth and I were dating. I used to sit on my couch and channel surf, and when I came across a Sally Struthers' commercial seeking funds to aid impoverished children in developing countries, I would keep on changing channels. Something very stupid and selfish would enter my mind, too. I would say to myself, "That's their problem, they should deal with their own, we should deal with ours." The hypocrisy of it all was that I was not doing anything to help any of "our own", either. Plus, I soon realized how completely ignorant I was to the plight of children around the world. In the U.S., we have the richest poor in the world and a system in place that keeps massive numbers of children from falling through the cracks.

It was around this time that Elizabeth went to work in orphanages in China. When she returned and she shared her stories, God cracked my heart wide open.

It is here that I hang my hat. I may not become the world's greatest dad or the most patient husband. I may still be a jerk in several areas of my life, but I can sense that the work God has done on this one part of me is reflective of His power to change other parts too. I feel a bit like the woman in the New Testament who grabbed hold of just a piece of Jesus' clothing and became healed. While it would be nice to embrace all of Jesus along with every bit of what He can do to change me, for now, I'll settle for this one piece that has given me the ability and strength to follow the James 1:27 command to "look after widows and orphans in their distress."

Also, while away in a far off distant land, in an uncomfortable setting, with a language barrier and completely different culture (in other words, a total interruption to the comforts I have set up for myself back home), and despite being who I am (a jerk), I still get to identify in part with God. For it is He who stepped down from a comfy throne in Paradise and crossed time and space in order to adopt us as His children. I am thankful that He didn't look at us and say, "That's their problem, they should deal with it." Instead, He looked at us - helpless, lost, alone and abandoned - and He loved us enough to make the trip.

So, to recap: My wife is amazing. I'm a jerk. But, thank God, He is not done working on me yet. And for now, I'll settle for identifying with Christ - by adopting another life into our family, our third child, Shea, from Ukraine. I just hope little Shea is not expecting Mr. Brady as his new dad!

13

Shea

For fun, to keep themselves occupied or simply out of curiosity, some women peruse the pages of magazines like *Good Housekeeping, Cosmopolitan* or *Redbook*. Not my wife. I don't think she has ever even had a magazine subscription in her life. Instead, Elizabeth surfs the internet looking at children around the world who are in need of parents. And, as she had done when she found Danielle, she was doing it again.

This time, she came across a little four-year-old boy from Ukraine named Shea. Shea was what you call cognitively typical, but he had Spina Biffida. This is a birth condition in which one is born with part of their spinal cord exposed. Surgery is required almost immediately in order to cover the cord back up. It often times causes paralysis. A shunt is placed near the skull in order to drain spinal fluid properly to keep it from entering the brain area. The effects are wide ranging. For Shea, all we knew at this time was that he might not have been able to walk.

My wife also discovered that in Ukraine, if a child is not adopted by the age of four or five, they are often moved to an adult institution for the rest of their lives. When she inquired further about Shea, she was told that he would most likely be kept in his bed for the rest of his life, because they (the workers in the institution) would not want to deal with him.

So Elizabeth told me about this little boy and the situation he was in and I leaped into action. My heart ached, as did hers, and I knew exactly what we needed to do. We needed to advocate for this little guy. We could not let this awful thing happen to him! Immediately I turned to Facebook and began to post his picture and tell his story. I e-mailed all of my friends and pleaded for someone to come forward to adopt him. One carrot I was able to dangle out there was that two-thirds of his adoption costs had been raised by a wonderful ministry called Reece's Rainbow, an organization dedicated to finding families for orphans with disabilities around the world. They specialize in children with Down syndrome, but they include many others as well. On the Reece's Rainbow website, there is an account set up for each child listed. Anyone can donate any amount into the account, and the money is then used to help parents cover the costs of the adoption. Many had already given to Shea's account, thanks to the fundraising efforts of a woman named Joanna Penny.

I was a little bit disappointed to have not heard from anyone. Finally, Joey, the wife of the bass player from my band, e-mailed me asking for more information. She and her husband, Jeff Norsen, were very close friends to Elizabeth and I. In fact, for a short time they even lived upstairs from us in an apartment above our home. I was excited that perhaps they would become Shea's new parents. I couldn't think of a better couple! They already had a birth son, so I was thrilled that now they might experience the joy of adoption, the way Elizabeth and I already had.

That night I was at a monthly men's event at my church. Jeff was also there and we talked further about the possibility of him and Joey adopting Shea. He sounded serious and I couldn't wait to get home and tell Elizabeth the great news.

When I arrived home, Danielle and Simon were asleep and Elizabeth was sitting on the couch in our living room. I sat down across from her on the other couch. I excitedly shared with her the great news about Jeff and Joey and their interest in adopting Shea. I was surprised when she met my news not with smiles but with tears. I was speechless, yet the lights in my brain were beginning to turn on. She didn't want us to advocate for Shea. She believed God was telling us to adopt him!

How could this be? We already had two children. Our house is very tiny. There had been no increase in our income since even adopting our first. And, by the way, hadn't we done enough? We couldn't save the world! Where could we draw the line? These and dozens of other questions and protests arose in my mind. Not to mention the fact that we would be in for a very awkward conversation with Jeff and Joey, who I believed were becoming more and more emotionally attached to the idea of adopting Shea.

Elizabeth convinced me to at least call Joey that night and tell her and Jeff that we, too, were considering Shea to become part of our family. I hadn't decided in the affirmative yet, but we wanted a little time to decide if we were going to pursue this or not. We didn't want the Norsens to become even more emotionally invested, so I made the call. Boy, was that uncomfortable. They took it well, but I could sense the disappointment in Joey's voice. I knew her heartstrings had been plucked and it was all my fault for not using my mind reading powers that all men are born with in order to pick up on what my wife really wanted. Oh yeah, that's right. We aren't actually born with any such powers, but it was still my fault!

A couple of days later, I was still in turmoil about the whole thing. At one point I turned to my wife and said, "We don't have the time. We don't have the money or the space. I don't have the energy. How can we possibly do this?"

She said, "Honey, I know all of that and all of that is true. But all I know is that God doesn't call the equipped, He equips the called."

I stopped dead in my tracks. She must have heard that saying at some Christian event she had attended. And for some reason, it hit me like a ton of bricks. Those blasted Women of Faith Conferences! That phrase rolled over in my mind again and again. And, above all, because of our previous adoptions, for which I felt totally inadequate both times, I knew it was true. God had equipped us when He called us. We never once got all of our ducks in a row before God decided to use us. We were about to adopt a third child!

So once again Elizabeth made the necessary calls and started the paperwork. Once again I was nervous. Two children had a sometimes exhausting effect on me. What would three do? But that dumb phrase kept rolling around and around in my head, "God doesn't call the equipped, He equips the called." Once again, those blasted Women of Faith!

And, once again, I called Jeff and Joey. Sheepishly I told them what should have been great news. They took it well, and despite their disappointment, they gave me the gift of affirming the strength of our friendship and offering their support for our decision.

And, once again, like players in a grand comedy, we witnessed yet another comically God moment from the Grand Director. A few days after officially committing to adopting Shea, my wife found out...wait for it...wait for it... she was pregnant!

Were we nervous? You bet.

Just as we had feared could happen, the orders by the Ukrainian officials to have Shea moved to an adult institution had gone through. And this was even after we had agreed to adopt him! Now we felt like we were racing the clock without the pace being set by us. Every small delay seemed to have possibly devastating consequences. Like when some of our official paperwork was held up by some inept employees at Fed-Ex. Shea had not yet been moved from his orphanage. If he was relocated before we arrived there to receive him, we were told we may not ever be able to get him out.

Our upcoming trip to Ukraine made me even more apprehensive than our first trip to China. It would be different in that we would not be going with a travel group. It would just be us. I pictured a harsh people with thuggish attitudes. Lots of smoking and run-down buildings. I must have seen these stereotypes in action movies featuring Eastern European Mafia types. My common sense told me not to pay attention to the stereotypes in my mind, as life was rarely like the movies anyway.

When we arrived in Ukraine, I was surprised after a time to see that it was a country filled with harsh people with thuggish attitudes, lots of smoking and rundown buildings. And one additional characteristic - for the most part, with a few exceptions, they really seemed to dislike Americans. In China, whether or not they like Americans is beside the point. The Chinese people try very hard to be good hosts and to serve visitors to their land. Here, we were met with much disdain, sometimes with gruff responses when we would go shopping. But mostly, people ignored us as much as they possibly could. The first time I got out of our driver's car, he rolled down his window and yelled at us. The interpreter told us that I closed his car door too hard! We were going to be with this guy for two weeks. Elizabeth and I decided to smother him with kindness and by the end of the first week, we could witness a bit of softening towards us. Especially since we always tried to tip generously.

I was again thankful to Reece's Rainbow for understanding the culture and the tone of the country, and providing us with just the right people to help us navigate these foreign waters. One aspect of life there that I could appreciate was that the men didn't really dress up. When we met one of the head contacts from Reece's Rainbow who was handling our case, he looked like something, well, out of an Eastern European Mafia action movie.

We met Ivan at our first official appointment at a government building. The first thing I noticed was that he wore a black shirt similar to what I would wear, but unbuttoned down to his naval. He chain-smoked, too. My wife pointed out that he bore some similarities to me. Short cropped hair (OK, balding) and heavy set. Although we didn't speak Ukrainian, it was evident as we met with various officials in the government offices that Ivan would flirt with the female bureaucrats in order to make our business run smoother. I liked watching him at work, and was also glad he was working for us and not against us. I imagined myself ending up with my feet in concrete at the bottom of the river with my ear being mailed to my family back home to "send a message" if I were to ever cross him. I know, I have a pretty active imagination.

The adoption requirements for Ukraine were different than those of China, too. China required a two-week trip. Ukraine required two two-week trips. The first one with both of us, the second with just one of us. Elizabeth was the natural choice to make both of the journeys, but one thing made that a bit difficult. She was pregnant. Very pregnant. About seven months pregnant.

This caused concern for two reasons. First, if we weren't scheduled for that second trip back to Eastern Europe in a timely manner, I would have to be the one to go. Elizabeth was determined to be the one to go, as close to her due date as needed, but there would most definitely be a point of no return where it would become unsafe for her and our child inside of her. I'm a fairly competent guy, but not nearly as familiar with all of the ins and outs of the bureaucracy we needed to go through in order to complete an adoption. Elizabeth was very on top of all that and knew exactly which appointments were needed to be completed and which paperwork we could not leave the country without. Like I said, I think I'm fairly competent, but in the end, still a guy. It would have caused great distress if I somehow managed to return to the U.S. with the wrong child, don't you think?

Our other concern was this: unlike China, Ukraine did not have a requirement preventing pregnant women from adopting. However, there were income requirements. We were concerned that with my already low level of income (I'm an artist remember), that the judge for our adoption hearing might not rule in our favor if he knew that we were about to add another child to our family. So Elizabeth hid her belly as best as she could. With her tall frame, she was fairly successful in doing this. We didn't tell anyone while we were there, although I think some of the women we dealt with suspected. We also hoped nobody would ask us flat out, as we didn't want to be caught in a lie.

We had to take an overnight train to Crimea to get to Shea's orphanage. This was an adventure for me, as I had never been on a real train trip before. We had our own room on the car and I was excited. Not the ideal situation for Elizabeth, however.

When we arrived, we were taken to our next apartment, which was on the fifth floor with no elevator. We had to hike it up those steps multiple times each day, and like so much of the trip had been, again not an ideal situation for my wife. However, I could see what a strong motivator love can be, especially in the heart of a mother. She endured all of the discomforts of our journey with such strength and dignity. I could not have been more proud.

The next day after our arrival, we were driven to Shea's orphanage. This was a huge building tucked away off from the road. It was surrounded by well-kept grounds. After being escorted inside, we were eventually led to our soon-to-be son's section of the massive structure. A staff person walked into the room where we were waiting, and she was carrying our new boy. He lit up the room, grinning from ear to ear. He had an infectious giggle and spoke a mile a minute in Russian. We gave him a teddy bear and he laughed contagiously. It looked as if we were going to get along just fine.

Our first visit was brief and then we were off to other parts of the orphanage to meet with different staff. When we met with the doctor, my wife had all sorts of technical questions about Shea's physical conditions. Because of her expertise as a physical therapist, her questions and follow up questions were quite complex. I wondered if the staff was impressed with this. As many of the hardened people we had met there, they held their cards close to their chest and remained very serious most of the time.

For the next ten days, twice per day, we journeyed from our apartment to the orphanage to spend time with Shea. These were the rules set up by the orphanage and we remained faithful in order to make a strong showing in court near the end of the week.

We would eventually have to go to court and plead our adoption case before a judge. This was an intimidating scenario because of the hardened nature of almost everyone we met. I couldn't imagine what it would be like to be on trial before a judge. And what if the judge did not rule in our favor and our entire trip had been for nothing? Or worse yet, what if Shea would be lost to an institution forever?

Shea was a delight. He was filled with energy and smiles. He loved the snacks we brought to him. Many of the staff had commented to us how intelligent he was. In fact, one person told us they felt he was one of the smartest children in the entire orphanage. I was fascinated to watch him converse with adults on the grounds of the facility. He would speak in Russian and appear to have very advanced conversations with passersby, such as gardeners and maintenance men. They seemed to speak with him as if he was a peer. Hearing Russian roll off of his lips was much fun.

The two trips to see Shea each day consisted of spending time with him indoors in a playroom or outside on the playground. We tried to be as creative as possible with our time with him, but we couldn't wait to get him home so we could provide him with all new experiences and adventures, and also so we could be his parents and not entertainers.

Our adoption hearing finally came. Elizabeth and I dressed up. She especially wanted to hide her pregnant belly from the judge who would hold all of the power to decide whether or not Shea could become the newest member of the Kulp family. I was quite nervous. After much waiting in a crowded hallway in the courthouse, we were finally called into the courtroom. Accompanied by our interpreter, we were instructed not to address her when asked a question, and to stand up whenever the judge asked us a question. Great, more things for me to screw up.

Also present in the court were three or four court appointed witnesses who sat alongside the judge. The orphanage was represented by a lawyer who sat with the orphanage psychologist and a social worker. There was also a prosecutor for the state. She really made me nervous, as I wasn't sure if her job was to argue against us being able to adopt Shea.

We stood and answered questions from the judge, the witnesses and the prosecutor for almost two hours. This was intense. Once again I was struck by the hard nature of the Ukrainians who seemed even harder in this setting.

Elizabeth's belly was blocked by a podium which stood between her and the judge; that was a relief. But at one point I saw one of the female representatives from the orphanage eyeball Elizabeth's tummy and suddenly lean over to another rep and whisper. As soon as she did this, they both looked again at Elizabeth. I knew that as women, they probably had picked up on our secret. I feared that when it was their turn, one of them would ask Elizabeth straight out, "Are you pregnant?" Had they asked, I wasn't sure how things would go down. It could jeopardize our entire case if the judge felt we could not financially afford to have four children in our family.

For me, the length of the hearing seemed to drag on forever. I felt like I was back in high school and standing in the principal's office defending my latest shenanigan. Elizabeth was much calmer, and I would later find out this was due to the fact that our judge was a very handsome man. While I felt like a suspect in an interrogation, she was enjoying the view. I suppose if the one in the robe had looked like Angelina Jolie, I may have been more at ease, too. No such luck.

The judge went through every piece of paperwork which sat in a tall stack in front of him. We had been informed that although he was an experienced judge, this was his first adoption case and he would probably want to make sure every "t" was crossed and every "i" was dotted. Boy, did he ever. Much of this seemed to me like overkill.

Part of the discussion centered on the boyfriend of Shea's birth mother. She had already surrendered full custody to the State, but while her boyfriend was in prison, he tried to make a play for custody. He wasn't even the birth father.

Our interpreter felt this wasn't very serious but was an attempt to bolster a possible parole case. Yet another facet to the story that concerned me, however, as I didn't want some ex-con traveling the high seas someday to come and take Shea away. The judge methodically nipped that in the bud.

When every piece of paper in that pile had been diligently examined and discussed, the judge announced a recess while he made his decision. So we waited.

After about another forty-five minutes, the judge reentered the courtroom. He quickly announced his ruling that Elizabeth and I were now Shea's legal parents. The stress was over. At the close of the hearing, we stood as the judge stepped down from the bench along with the witnesses. He approached us and for the first time since we first saw him, he gave us a wide and warm smile and gregariously shook our hands. Through our interpreter he said some incredibly kind things about Elizabeth and I and how thrilled he was that we were Shea's parents now. The government witnesses expressed the same.

After all of the intensity and seriousness, not just in the courthouse but during most of our stay, we were finally experiencing a kinder and gentler side from the Ukrainians. I realized too that, as uncomfortable as it had all been, the people who stood before us now - the judge, witnesses, attorneys, social workers, orphanage director and psychologists - had all been working as hard as they could on behalf of little Shea. Ultimately, they wanted what we wanted, a good home and loving parents for this young orphan who already had so many cards stacked against him. I was now appreciative of how they dotted every "i" and crossed every "t."

Emily

Elizabeth made the required trip back to Ukraine to pick up Shea. It would be another two week venture, but this time her parents would be going along to help while I stayed home with Danielle and Simon. She was even more pregnant than before. There was no hiding it this time around, but it didn't matter. We were Shea's legal parents. She was cutting it very close to the point of no return.

A few weeks after coming home with Shea, Elizabeth gave birth to little Emily Carol Kulp. She was a bright eyed, dark haired beauty. On the second night after the birth, our three other children were brought to the hospital by Simon and Danielle's godparents, Vinnie and Judy, to see their new little sister. I'll never forget the image of Simon walking up to Emily, who was in her mother's arms, and gently stroking her head and giving her a big kiss. As Simon is non-verbal, his way of saying "I love you" has always been to tenderly touch your forehead. She had officially been welcomed into the family by her oldest brother.

God gave us the perfect little girl to join our family. Emily is easy going, fun-loving and usually wears the cutest of smiles upon her face. Her "go with the flow" spirit is a huge relief. I'm not sure what we would do if she wasn't so low-maintenance.

Danielle, Simon and Shea simply adore her. Each one expresses this love in their own uniquely stamped gestures, too. I mentioned how Simon softly caresses her forehead. Shea chases her around our living room in a goofy game of tag. Danielle prefers to hold her, stand her up, sit her down, lift her up by her arms, and tickle her. We keep a close eye, but usually Emily endures all of this with giggles and a smile.

Every once in a while we lament how perhaps Emily is being cheated out of the extra attention she deserves because of all of the focus placed on the others' special needs. But then, I watch how joyfully she interacts with her brothers and sister, and also remember the gift my own parents gave me with my adopted siblings, and I stop worrying. "She'll be just fine," I think to myself. "In fact, she'll be better than fine!"

From my own experiences I know her journey in this family won't always be easy, but I also know that she will have the blessing of being touched by special needs in a way most people never get to have. And, like me sitting in that restaurant in China, I can only hope the warm memories of her upbringing that flood her mind someday as an adult will include warm feelings for her mother and I. I hope the legacy I leave her, and am leaving her even now, is accepted and lived out just as my father's was in my life.

In other words, I pray little Emily grows up one day to adopt orphans, too! Orphans with special needs would also be out of this world. But this is her journey to discover. I just know that even now, the seeds are at least being planted as she gets a front row seat to the chaos which ensues in our home, and, someday, she will have a much longer chapter in a future book. Her pages have yet to be filled.

The Face of God

My father used to say that sometimes looking into the face of a child with Down syndrome was like looking into the face of God. I believe he was right.

Years ago when I worked for a Presbyterian church as a youth director, I would attend a Christmas service held by an outside organization that ran group homes for the developmentally disabled. Dozens of residence and the staff from their individual homes would arrive, many with wheel chairs, representing a variety of diagnoses. To an outside world, unfamiliar with special needs, this service may have seemed like a noisy, chaotic free for all. Loud voices could be heard at "inappropriate times". Movement abounded as people rocked back and forth in their seats. Some drooled. Some yelled. The Christmas songs were a cacophony of off key singing, moans and unintelligible lyrics. This was not your ordinary worship service. And yet, I never felt closer to God in church than at those services.

One year, the pastor asked if I would like to deliver the sermon. I was honored. Friends, never turn down an opportunity to experience worship with the "least" among us. You will be blessed.

This idea should not be new to us. Jesus made it very clear to us that a connection with Him often comes in the least likely places. In Matthew 25:40, Jesus says, "I tell you the truth, whatever you did for one of the least of these brothers of mine, you did for me." Here, Jesus was talking about the hungry, the thirsty, strangers and prisoners. I am pretty confident, however, that people with special needs fits His criteria of a gathering of people where He can be found.

Growing up, I was often amazed at the seemingly "built in" spirituality of my brothers and sisters who had Down syndrome. I remember one time when we were kids watching the classic movie about Jesus Christ, "The Greatest Story Ever Told", along with David, Suzanne, Sarah and Matthew. I wasn't sure how much they could really understand of the story until the crucifixion scene. When Jesus died on the cross, I looked over and saw Sarah crying because Jesus had died. The others were also visibly mourning His death, too. Sarah was the most non-verbal of the bunch, so her tears were especially poignant. And, in glorious fashion, when Jesus was resurrected, there was an outcry of cheers, smiles, high-fives and celebrating as one of them yelled, "Jesus is back!"

Somehow, my brothers and sisters were able to glean far more from the story than I would have anticipated. They loved Jesus. I grew up with the feeling that they knew Jesus in a deeper and more profound way than I ever would, and based on far less head knowledge than me. It almost seems as though their knowledge is contained in the heart, planted there by their Creator. They may not ever be able to articulate the Gospel message using mere words, but the love they have for God is written all over their face.

Thus, sometimes when my father looks into the eyes of a child with Down syndrome, it is like looking into the face of God.

Dan and Matthew Kulp then...

And now.

Dan with his brothers David and Matthew and sisters Sarah and Suzanne
in the winter of 1980.

Norm and Carol Kulp with three of their nine children:
Suzanne, Sarah and Matthew.

Elizabeth working with children in an orphanage in China.

The Dig Project live in concert in Rochester, NY.

Belting it out with his band at the Pro-life Music fest in Indiana.

Moments after leaving his orphanage forever,
Simon falls asleep safely in Elizabeth's arms.

Snuggling with Grandpa Kulp.

Simon plays with his Uncle David.

He may be non-verbal - but Simon loves to talk to his Father.

Danielle meets her new Mommy for the very first time.

Dan shakes the hand of the man who found Simon abandoned in the woods.

Danielle readies herself for her first race in the Special Olympics.

Danielle with her Grandma Button.

Shea swimming with family and friends.

He ain't heavy- he's my brother.

The boys go riding with Grandpa Button.

He's got a trail to blaze.

Both sets of grandparents with all four kids.

Trying to be a good daddy for Emily...or at least a good doggie.

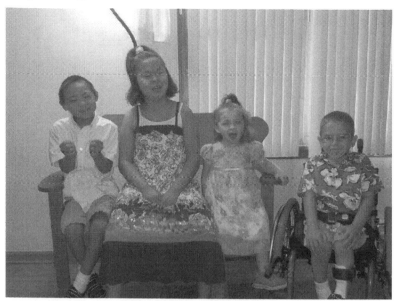

Simon, Danielle, Emily and Shea.

Dan and Matthew with their Mom and Dad.

Dan's treasure.

Flesh and Blood

I hear a lot of objections as to why people won't adopt, and to be honest, most of them are poor excuses. One of these that I find most difficult to relate to goes something like this:

"I'm not sure I could love a child that is not my own."

Sometimes it is not expressed in such a straight forward manner, but I hear that it is a common concern.

Not that I have any statistical proof of what I am about to say, but based on my own family experience as well as the many adoptive parents I have spoken with, if this is your concern, you need not worry. You may think that it is unnatural to love a child to whom you did not give birth. I say it is just the opposite. If you make the life changing, God honoring decision to adopt a young life into your family, let me assure you that it would be unnatural to not love that child as your own.

This is because adoption is not simply a physical act. It is a spiritual action where God provides for one of His own by grafting a parentless child into a brand new family. God's plan of adoption has been around for thousands of years and I think He is pretty excited about the whole thing. Moses was adopted. His new situation allowed him to lead his people out of slavery in Egypt, eventually leading to the

Promised Land and paving the way for the Savior of all mankind. Imagine if Pharaoh's daughter had thought, "Gee, I don't know if I can love this little baby I found floating down the river. Maybe someone else should do it."

Jesus was also adopted by Joseph. Pretty weird situation, too, I might add. You know, Mary being impregnated by the Ruler of the Universe and all. Yet, God made it work.

And because God made it work, He also makes it work for us to be adopted into His family! Imagine that. We were hopeless and helpless lying in a spiritual dying room until God "first loved us" and made a way for us to be adopted into His family through His Son Jesus Christ.

When I was growing up, every once in a while I would be asked something like, "So how many real brothers and sisters do you have?" Very early on, I learned to say, "Well, they're all my real brothers and sisters." And quite frankly, that is how I've always felt. For me, there has never really been a difference between my three adopted siblings and my five biological brothers and sisters. They have always felt the same. Sure, I am closer to some than others, but I love them all.

Same goes for my children. Although we gave birth to little Emily, her brothers and sister hold the same status as full-fledged Kulps as she does. This is not to say that when you first adopt that there may not be some sort of adjustment period. I've already told about my struggle bonding with Danielle in the beginning. However, I've never felt, even during the rocky beginning, that she wasn't a real Kulp or that I didn't truly love her. I also know many people who have an adjustment period when they first give birth to their biological children. Hey, it's quite a life change to all of a sudden have a new person in your life who looks to you as Mom or Dad and depends on you for pretty much everything. One who changes your schedule. Invades your space. Wakes you up in the middle of the night.

I once saw a documentary called "My Flesh and Blood" (2003) about a woman who has taken in several children, many with special needs. At one point in an interview, she called these kids her "flesh and blood". I know exactly how she feels.

I even forget sometimes that Simon, for example, did not actually come from my loins. We will go out to a grocery store or other public place and every once in a while someone will ask when we adopted him. My first thought is often, "How did they know?" I actually forget that he is Asian and we obviously look different from one another! There is not a single ounce of me that loves him any less because we did not deliver him in a delivery ward at the hospital. He is my son, with whom I am well pleased.

Years ago, I would occasionally be called upon to give a talk, deliver a message or preach a sermon on adoption. I didn't have any biological children or adopted children, but I guess because of my adopted brothers and sisters I was considered qualified. I would open with the same joke which I absolutely loved but can no longer use. Standing in front of my audience, I would say, "Now, I haven't adopted any children," then hoisting up my pants by the belt buckle and with a smug look on face would say, "at least none that I know about." That one is up for grabs.

It's Funny on TV, Right?

I've already mentioned that when my brother Matthew was born, the doctors called him "Mongoloid." That was not an unkind description at the time. It is now, however. In fact, he was also called "mentally retarded." This, too, was not considered politically incorrect. The word "retard" has usually been meant as sort of a derogatory term, even back in the seventies. Now, it is as morally reprehensible as using the word "nigger," at least to the special needs community.

Growing up, I heard this term often, usually in three contexts. I would say most in the developmentally disabled communities have also had the same experience.

The first is said directly to or about the person who is mentally challenged. It is a vile and demeaning insult meant to degrade the recipient. I am happy to report that I witnessed very little of this trash talk towards my family growing up. The times I did were few and far between. I can remember getting in a fist fight with one of our town bullies because he called my brother David a "retard". However, most people didn't dare utter the word in our presence. I always had the sense, though, that behind our backs this may have happened much more frequently.

If I were to see this with my own two eyes today, mercy would not be my first response. Pastor Dan would quickly become just Dan and I would have very little sympathy for the person on the other end of my fist. Sorry, just the way I feel. Not saying it is the godliest of attitudes or the most theologically correct attitude to have, just saying it is the way I am. Can't stand bullies.

The second context the word "retard" is used today is out of sheer ignorance. It is used as slang and as a substitute word. Teenagers aren't the only ones who do it, but I do hear them do it more than others. I have almost twenty years of youth ministry experience, working with both churched and unchurched kids. Phrases like "She is so retarded!" or "You're such a retard" were often heard. The person uttering these things usually isn't thinking much about it. They are replacing words like "idiot" and "moron" with the "R-word."

I heard this a lot as a kid. For whatever reason, it didn't bother me that much, as long as it wasn't directed towards someone who actually did have a mental challenge. Don't get me wrong. I'm not saying it is the proper word usage. I never did this myself, out of sensitivity to my own siblings. But I also didn't get too worked up about it when I heard it in the halls of my school. I don't get too worked up about it now, either. I realize that most of time there is no malice involved. Ignorance, yes. Malice, not usually. I do understand that many in the special needs communities find it harmful and hurtful in any context. I simply have chosen not to be offended.

For me, people's intentions are what it's all about. I was in a Facebook group for parents of children with special needs when someone posted an experience they had at a Walmart.

A mother was walking into the store with their child with Ds when an elderly employee standing near the entrance greeted them. He noticed the child and brought up how he knew someone who had a dog with Down syndrome. The parent was "offended" and went on Facebook to express her outrage. She was joined on her post by like-minded individuals who decried this man's insensitivity.

I think I may have been one of the only ones who looked at the whole thing from a different perspective. From the scenario described, it seemed as though the gentleman was being kindly. He didn't seem to intend to be hurtful in anyway. I thought perhaps he was just trying to build a bridge. Find common ground. I think my reaction would have been, instead of being offended, to engage even more in conversation about Down syndrome. To be honest, I have never heard of a dog with Down syndrome. I still don't know if that is real or not, but I think it is pretty neat. I would have said "Wow!" and asked questions like, "Was the dog delayed in any way?" "Was it more affectionate than most typical dogs?" "What were its behaviors like?" The situation could have also have been used to educate this individual about Ds in a child. Sometimes in life, it is best to choose not to be offended.

The third context is through our entertainment and media. You don't know how often I have seen a parent of a child with special needs post on Facebook their hurt and frustration after going to see their favorite stand-up comedian and their liberal use of the "R-word". Again, most of the time, I simply shrug it off as ignorance on the part of the performer. I don't like it and I don't find it particularly funny, but as I've said before, I simply choose to not be offended. If it happens to be a routine about someone with disabilities, then not only is it not funny, but it is at this point that I find it offensive. I mean come on, let's pick on our most vulnerable members of society, who often don't have the means or voice to speak up for themselves, and mock their very existence? You gotta be a cold-hearted SOB with a complete lack of compassion (not to mention creativity) to think a routine like that is funny or morally acceptable. I say the same to those who laugh and think said comedian is funny.

Usually this experience for a parent happens in concert with other incidents, which makes it all the more hurtful. Think about it. You send your child off to school and find out that a kid on the bus called your beloved child a retard. Then you find out the same thing happened at school. Each cutting incident causes your soul to weep. You love your child. In fact, you don't even see their "disability" any more. You just see the apple of your eye. Your child, with whom you are well pleased and would die for. The one for whom you would take upon your own shoulders every infirmity they may ever have, if you could. And then some cruel child demeans your little one.

Later on that night, after a hard day of tears and contemplating why children have to be so unkind, you turn on the TV seeking some escape from it all. You stop on a channel featuring some stand-up comedians. A laugh is what you could use right now... and BAM. There it is. The comedian drops the "R-word" three times during their routine. They didn't do a routine about the intellectually challenged, they just used it for effect or to accent a joke. Out of ignorance. It doesn't matter though. Your child comes to mind. You picture their beautiful face. You imagine the other children calling them a retard. And you are angry and offended. And you also wonder if this is where kids learn such words. I mean, it's funny on TV right?

There is a movement in some segments of the special needs communities now to use what is called "People First Language". For example, you are not supposed to say, "Down syndrome child" anymore. But, instead, you are to say, "a child who has Down syndrome." No more, "autistic kids" and "special needs children", but instead, "a child who has autism" or a "a child with special needs." You get the picture. My question is, two of my children are from China. Should I refer to them as "my two children who have Chinese?"

Wolves in Sheep's Clothing

As I said earlier, when someone says something offensive I usually try not to be offended. It's a big waste of time.

But this was different.

It was late at night, and I had been watching "The Tonight Show." Jay Leno has always been a favorite of mine, but tonight I turned off the TV feeling sort of stunned. On March 19th, 2008, "The Tonight Show's" special guest made a mockery of thousands upon thousands of people with special needs when he said, with laughter, that his bowling score of 129 was "like the Special Olympics or something".

It seemed to roll off his tongue so easily that I wondered if it was a barb he used all the time with buddies on the basketball court. Why would he mock the athletes of the Special Olympics with such an unfunny joke? Leno handled the situation as best he could, basically ignoring the immature comment.

We all have certain words that give us warm feelings whenever we hear them. For some, it might be the words "Disney World", "The Andy Griffith Show", "Star Wars", "hot cocoa by a warm fire" (I started to write "chocolate" but then realized "cocoa" sounds even more warm and cozy, am

I right?), or "Keanu Reeves" Hey, I don't know. It's different for everybody.

The words "Special Olympics" definitely have this effect on me. When I was younger, the Special Olympics offered a place of acceptance for not only my siblings, but also for me. You see, I could go there and not feel as though people were whispering behind my back and telling little jokes about us. I didn't have to worry about what other kids thought or how my family was being judged. I also got to witness my brothers and sisters being celebrated for their efforts. Years ago, you could even volunteer to be a "hugger" at the Special Olympics games. Your job was to stand at the finish line and give a huge hug to the athletes when they finished their race. It was a beautiful sight.

Another beautiful sight I often witnessed: when a runner would fall, all of the other runners would stop and wait for them to get back up, and then everyone would continue the race. How cool would our world be if we looked out for one another like that? Don't get me wrong, I am all for healthy competition and "going for the gold". But I've always been struck by the pure and unadulterated love these athletes had for one another.

So growing up, the Special Olympics was a huge part of my life. David, Suzanne, Matthew and Sarah were very active participants competing in track and field, swimming, floor hockey and many other events, including bowling. In fact, my daughter Danielle has also competed in the bowling Special Olympics.

So when, during the interview on "The Tonight Show", the guest showed his lack of respect for these wonderful competitors, I was angry. I felt like I did when I was a kid, wanting to stand up to the bully who would attempt to degrade my brothers and sisters because they were different. Why did this incident strike me with such disdain when I might otherwise just blow off his remark? Because, the guest who was making the joke was the President of the United States, Barack Obama.

He's not the first to use our special children as an insult to others. In 1994, then Vice President Al Gore attacked supporters of Oliver North, who was running for the Senate in Virginia, by calling them "the extreme right wing, the extra chromosome right wing." Hmm. Who do you think Al was referring to? There is more than one genetic condition which involves an extra chromosome, but all of them include mental and physical challenges. The most common is Down syndrome. He was most likely trying to make fun of his political opponents by comparing them to people who have Ds. This is yet another example of someone whose insensitive comments show contempt for the special needs community.

I believe this type of degradation of our children is more insidious than a cheap shot by an entertainer or the ignorant teen who uses "the R-word", because people in power have the potential to contribute far more to the devaluing of human life.

When our leaders in society behave this way, where does it all lead? If I had my way, it would lead to their careers being plopped onto the dung heap of history and relegated to a Trivial Pursuit question. (Do people still play that game?)

But let me direct your attention to Britain.

In 2013, British politician Colin Brewer stunned the public when he compared disabled children - my children, by the way - to misshapen lambs sometimes killed by farmers. In an article in the Huffington Post UK, Brewer is quoted as telling the Disabled News Network, "If they [the farmers] have a misshapen lamb, they get rid of it. They get rid of it. Bang...We are just animals...You can't have lambs running around with five legs and two heads. It would be put down, smashed against the wall and be dealt with."

Or maybe he didn't stun the entire public, because he was reelected!

As I sit here writing, I'm remembering a scene from yesterday which played out in my own living room. Danielle was joyfully singing along to her favorite musical on DVD. Shea was enthusiastically helping to clean up our living room of scattered toys so it would be more presentable for Mommy. And for no particular reason, Simon walked up to Emily and lovingly wrapped his arm around her and gently kissed her forehead, just like he did when they met for the very first time. I can't help think about a government bureaucrat comparing my children to misshapen lambs not worthy of breathing the breath of life.

Let me ask you something: who is more valuable to society? A child with special needs, even a child with the most severe or complex needs, who enriches the lives of everyone he touches? Who brings countless smiles and unspeakable joy to friends, neighbors, parents and siblings, and makes us a more feeling and compassionate society? Or the career politician who takes far more from the people than he will ever be able to give back?

I think many politicians have been sheltered in government jobs for so long they rarely, if ever, rub shoulders with someone with mental challenges for longer than a photo-op. Their loss. But the little sirens go off in my head when a person in a powerful position just doesn't seem to get it, because history has shown us that an offhand comment here and a seemingly innocent joke there can lead to dire consequences.

In his quest to engineer the perfect German race, Adolph Hitler was murdering the disabled through his Operation T-4 euthanasia program before moving on to the Jews. According to the Jewish Virtual Library, up to 250,000 mentally and physically disabled were murdered in Germany between 1939 and 1945.

And despite the efforts of revisionist historians, let us not forget that Margaret Sanger, the founder of Planned Parenthood, started the agency to eliminate the black population as well as, you guessed it, the disabled. In fact, check out this quote by Sanger from one of her articles in November of 1923:

"The object of civilization is to obtain the highest and most splendid culture of which humanity is capable. But such attainment is unthinkable if we continue to breed from the present race stock that yields us our largest amount of progeny. Some method must be devised to eliminate the degenerate and the defective; for these act constantly to impede progress and ever increasingly drag down the human race."

Nice. There seems to be little difference between the efforts of Planned Parenthood and the Nazi gas chambers. Can you see now why a joke made in jest by a politician on a late night talk show can set me off?

I have to wonder if Obama truly values all human life any more than Brewer or Margaret Sanger? His remark on "The Tonight Show" aside, as an Illinois State Senator, President Obama voted four times against the Born Alive Infant Protection Act (BAIPA), which would have made it a crime to murder children who survived abortions. He now has implemented the most sweeping government power grab in our history with his ill-conceived Obamacare. Without respect for human life, all human life, and with bureaucrats at the helm, what happens when the money runs out? Who decides who is and isn't worthy of medical care?

As a father of three children with special needs who have very good health coverage (coverage that Elizabeth and I have made great sacrifices and worked very hard for), I'm afraid there will soon be a price on their heads if the government ever completely takes over our health care system.

The irony is that many of our disabled citizens will overcome great odds to become contributing, tax-paying, members of society and will surely feed the corrupt government machine these politicians live off.

I know I sound angry. That's because I am. Most people have no idea the battles parents fight on behalf of children with special needs. These can include fighting with school districts over what is best for their children (because in many places in the country, again, the bureaucrats think they know better), arguing with insurance companies about crucial medical attention a child needs, or simply figuring out a way to get a wheel chair in and out of a poorly accessible building.

The list is endless. Having to deal with people in power who hold many of the cards played against our children is a sad reality for us.

Want to compare my kids to sheep? Guess what – when sheep are bitten by a wolf, we grab a shotgun and hunt down the wolf and eliminate it. And just in case this gets read by some tax payer funded federal employee at the NSA or Department of Homeland security: I am not advocating violence towards the President or any other politician. By this point in the book, you should have figured out that I value human life. In fancy writer's lingo, what I just said is an analogy. That means that I didn't literally mean anyone should grab a shotgun and eliminate anything. In this case "eliminating" the wolf means voting these elitists out of office. So please, no black helicopters at my house.

19

More Than a Lot

I learned two great lessons about kids: Children are awesome. Wonderful. Life-changing. A blessing.

And very, very gross.

I had absolutely no idea what I was in for when I became a dad. My wife still makes fun of me for the time I had to bring Simon to the potty while at a family gathering at my parents' house. While on the toilet, he ended up peeing on me. I was so grossed out that I left the family gathering and ran to a Big Lots store and bought $4.00 T-shirt. I knew I wouldn't be able to relax until I replaced my shirt. Elizabeth thinks I way over reacted. But this fatherhood thing was still pretty new to me. Sorry if I was unable to take getting peed on in stride! I've lived on this planet for almost forty years and I can say that I have never, ever been hit with urine. But since being a dad, I have regularly been peed on, sneezed on, pooped on and thrown up on.

And this is what I mean about children being gross. I had never even changed a diaper before we went to China that first time. Remember, initially I was number five out of six children. Everybody had to change my diaper.

I didn't even know that inside each and every disposable diaper was a gel-like substance that, when combined with urine, turns into a tapioca pudding-like concoction.

How did I find this out? One day I was watching Simon while Elizabeth was out. Nap time came and I brought him to his bedroom. As I was about to lay him down, he started tugging on his shirt, indicating he would like to sleep shirtless. Understandable, considering he was kept bundled up most of the time in his orphanage due to poor heating. So I pulled off his shirt. He then started tugging on his pants. I enjoy sleeping in my underwear, too, so no problem. I laid him down in his crib in just a diaper. Big mistake.

I kicked back in the living room and started watching TV, and I could hear him down the hall. He was laughing and jumping. Sounded like a party was going on. As if as soon as I left the room he called up some friends and said, "C'mon over and" …wait for it …wait for it… "check out my crib!" I know. Lame joke.

After a while I figured I had better go and see what was happening. I approached his bedroom and cracked open the door. As I peered in, I saw Simon standing there buck naked. He had ripped off his diaper like he was a Chippendale dancer and was tearing it into a thousand little pieces. This is when I first discovered the gel-like substance. He was tossing it everywhere. It looked like a ticker tape parade in my son's bedroom. It was in his hair, on the walls and all over the carpet!

Another time, as I stepped out of the shower and wrapped a towel around myself, I stepped into the hall and there stood Simon. He loves to wrestle, so I picked him up and brought him into my bedroom. I flopped down on my bed, hoisted him up over my head and…sploosh! He threw up right in my eye! Nothing more refreshing than throw up in the eye first thing in the morning. Shower ruined.

I could share story after story like these about all of my kids. If you're a parent, they really aren't that shocking. You have your own tales of great moments in grossness to tell. And, if you've been doing it a while, they aren't a big deal anymore.

A close friend of mine, who was about to become a dad for the first time, confided in me that the one thing making him nervous about his upcoming coronation into fatherhood was having to change diapers and dealing with poop. He was afraid of throwing up. I assured him he has nothing to worry about. Eventually, you become so bonded with your child you don't even think about it anymore. I told him it becomes like wiping your own butt. "Wiping yourself doesn't gross you out does it?" I asked. I'm happy to report he has three children and changes diapers like a pro.

This all leads me to the second lesson I've learned about fatherhood and it is far more important than "children are gross". No matter how gross they can be, how challenging, how disobedient, there has never been one part of me in all my being that has loved them any less. This was an incredible epiphany for me, because it made me think, "What if this is how God feels about me? What if there is nothing I can do to make God love me any less than He does right now? What if there is nothing I can do to make Him love me any more than He does right now?" Wow! What an incredible thing for me to learn in my late thirties about the character and nature of God's magnificent love for me. And I learned this incredible and profound message from my little boy Simon, who has both Down syndrome and Autism.

I've learned more about the great depth of God's love for me from being a dad, more than I ever learned in my years of ministry. And the lessons keep coming. Thank you, kids. Daddy loves you. In fact, I now ask my little Emily, "Emily, do you know how much I love you?" She used to answer "A lot", and I would say, "More than a lot!" Now she knows to answer, "More than a lot!"

When I was touring the country in a rock band for years (how cool does that sound?), I had high hopes and ambitions. Big dreams, man. I used to fantasize about getting to open up for a super group like U2. Or that one day, I would write that one hit song that would change the world. Now, I find myself writing songs like:

"There's a party on the potty
And poopie and pee pee are invited.
There's a party on the potty
And poopie and pee pee will be there.
You can tinkle on the toilet
And let everybody know it
They'll be delighted
There's a Party on the Potty
With something that smells different in the air."

A Wealthy Poor Man

I've lived a good life. My upbringing with my four brothers and sisters who have Down syndrome has given me a whole different set of experiences, a unique perspective than most, some additional challenges and a wonderful story to tell.

My life has not been easy, but it has not been difficult, either. I never suffered from abuse, struggled with drug addiction or been stricken with cancer. Growing up, my mother told me how she and my dad didn't have much money, but this was information I was pretty oblivious to. We lived in a large house with a swimming pool and always had enough food to eat and toys to play with. For the most part, all of us got along pretty well.

I was a Boy Scout, played baseball, delivered newspapers, worked odd jobs at the corner pizza shop, swam a lot and played outdoors quite often.

"Star Wars" changed my life and made me a lifelong movie nut. TV was a big thing in our house. My home was filled with music as my mother loved to sing and my father loved, loved, loved music of all kinds.

I wasn't the most popular kid in school, but I also wasn't unpopular. I loved high school because of the social element, but my grades were lackluster because of my love for the social element. I loved girls and had good female friendships, but didn't date much, as I lacked any sort of confidence to ask them out, due to being overweight. I wasn't a bad kid, but I was mischievous.

I had a lot of hopes and dreams when I was kid. Since I was five years old, I wanted to become an actor. I ate, breathed and slept movies. My life plan from five years old all the way to my senior year in high school was to, upon graduation, load up my car, drive to California, and try and get into movies. My parents were even supportive. I had often told my mom as a kid that I would one day be rich and famous and present her and my father with great and luxurious gifts in reward for being such terrific parents.

My guidance counselor in high school, Mrs. Stern, was beside herself that I was uninterested in college. My plan was more important and I was going to stick to it. Then, without warning, something changed. It was winter of my senior year and I was sitting in a youth group that I had been very active in called Young Life. Suddenly, I had this very strong feeling that I should not pursue acting, but youth ministry instead. At the time, I was convinced this was God speaking to my heart. Looking back, I'm not sure if it was just good old fashioned fear of failure which stopped me from loading up my little red '78 Chevette with all of my belongings and heading west. At the very least, I suppose I should have feared my car not making it all the way to the movie mecca of the galaxy. Either way, this decision led me down a completely different path.

I marched in to the guidance office that week and announced to Mrs. Stern that I decided to go to college after all. You would have thought I was her prince charming and had just walked in and presented her with a dozen roses. She was elated! She immediately began to bring out brochures and lists of majors at different colleges. I had absolutely no idea what I would pursue. One thing we both realized was that my choices were limited, as I skipped the SATs because I hadn't planned on going to college. Plus, I didn't want to get up early on a Saturday to take them.

So I decided to attend Monroe Community College (MCC), right in my own city. As we scanned the list of majors, I settled on Communications: Media/Arts. Although I really had no desire to be a radio DJ or news anchor, this was the closest thing I could find to the acting field. I would attend MCC, one of the top rated community colleges in the country, and eventually enter into full time youth ministry.

Another dream began to emerge when I graduated high school. I started a band with a friend of mine. I called the group Nobody's Fool, and I was the lead singer. Although we never really broke out of the Rochester music scene, we were still fairly well known in the area, as far as Christian rock bands go. During this time, I dreamed that one day, I would get to tour. I didn't care about making loads of money, having hit songs on the radio, or becoming famous. I only wanted to travel the country and play in a different place every night. Nobody's Fool had a six year run. It looked like I would never be in a touring band.

We ended after six years because I had met a girl. She became my first serious girlfriend. Eventually we married and moved to Michigan, so she could pursue her Master's Degree. Then, we moved to Florida where she pursued her Doctorate. Our plan was for me to pursue something meaningful, after she received her degrees and was making a load of money putting her Doctorate to good use with a dream job. During her schooling, I worked many different jobs for income. I worked as a waiter, banquet manager, chicken delivery driver, door to door survey taker, truck driver delivering truck accessories and a youth director. Then, after five years of this, she left. Met someone else. And I was devastated.

Every dream that I had, I had traded or put on hold to be with her. Now, I had nothing but an Associate's Degree in Media Arts. No wife, no money, no accomplishments. I felt like a colossal failure in life. I certainly wouldn't be bestowing lavish gifts upon my parents.

The day after I became aware of the events which lead to the demise of my marriage, I drove to my mother and father's house, still the home I had grown up in. I cried and shouted out to God all the way there. I sat in my parent's living room and broke down again. Sobbing, I said, "Five years. I couldn't make it five years. Five years and I have nothing to show for it. I'm a failure!"

In typical Norm Kulp fashion, Dad said, "Don't ever let me hear you say that. You are not a failure. If I hear you call yourself that again, I'm going to take you out back to the woodshed." We never had a woodshed. My father never took me to one. In fact, although dad had quite a bark, he rarely ever bit. I recall very few times he even spanked me. But I knew what he meant and was grateful for their encouragement on that devastating evening.

During this dark time in my life, some things started to happen. First, I met a guy named Mike at a church singles event at a bowling alley. He played guitar. I told him I had a bunch of songs I had written from my Nobody's Fool days, and needed a guitarist who could accompany me with these while I sang at coffee houses and churches. Eventually, we met some more musicians and turned our little acoustic act into a real life band. Opportunity after opportunity opened up and over about a three year period we saturated our local market. The logical next step for our band, which started out as D.I.G. (Death is Gain) and later became The Dig Project, was to tour. And, in a remarkable and probably way out of our league fashion, we did.

For about a year and a half I was completely lonely. Thankful for my band - Mike, Bill, and Jeff - but oh, so broken by the loss I was suffering daily. Songwriting and performing, as well as the camaraderie which comes from fellow musicians, provided some distraction from the pain as well as something to work for. This new group of friends in my life were like an antiseptic spray for a sore throat. They couldn't heal my sickness, but they sure brought a little pain relief.

Another source of relief was my oldest sister, Linda. She had been widowed for a few years and understood the sense of loss I was experiencing, even if from a different angle. She took me under her wing and would meet me for lunches and dinners and became a movie buddy, too. This big sister of mine is twelve years older than I am, and up until this point, often served in a role as sort of a second mom – changing my diapers and babysitting me when I was little, having me for overnights, as I was close to her son Joshua growing up, and even lecturing me about my behavior. We are on opposite ends of the political spectrum, too. But none of that mattered. Even though, at thirty years old, I sometimes felt like the nerdy kid who had to take his sister to the prom, when I was hurting Linda was a friend to me, and I will be forever grateful.

The loneliness factor was ever present though, and sometimes made me jealous of those around me. With rock bottom self-esteem, I longed to be with someone of the opposite sex who would love me, quirks, extra poundage and all. One time, our guitarist came to band practice very excited because some girl had seen him up front playing in the worship band at church and wanted to meet him. She made it known to a friend who made it known to him. They soon started dating.

Over dinner one night with Tony, my best friend from high school, I poured out my longings. "Why can't that happen to me?" I asked. "Why can't some girl see me up on stage and be impressed with who I am? That stuff never happens to me?" I wanted someone who would pursue me for a change. I felt that in my last relationship, I did most of the pursuing, and when she left, any sense of self-worth I may have had walked out the door with her.

At the year and a half mark something miraculous happened. I was sleeping on my futon. That's right, I said futon. That's what single dudes sleep on when they have to move in with their single band mates after a personal tsunami hits. I woke up one morning and had a sense of peace I never felt before. It was something that was so powerful and so satisfying. It was contentment. Specifically, contentment with being single. This was something I never experienced. And I don't mean just since my wife had left. I mean ever. Long before I was married, going all the way back to at least junior high school. I always wanted someone in my life. And now, for the first time ever, I didn't need female companionship to be happy. I laid there staring up at the ceiling and began to smile as I felt the burden of loneliness I had been carrying for so long float off my body and upward towards the ceiling. I laughed a joyful laugh. I realized my singleness was a gift. I no longer cared if I had a woman in my life or not. I was single and at complete and total peace.

Something changed in me that day. I felt whole. Now I was emotionally healthy rather than broken. And, wouldn't you know it, I started dating again - and I liked it!

Along comes the second great event.

The second great event occurred while we were performing at the Canandaigua United Methodist Church, near our home in Rochester. As I was on stage, I noticed a young lady in the audience. She was volunteering as a leader for the youth group up the road and consequently with the same church our bass player Jeff grew up in. And by the way, she noticed me, too. She would one day become my wife.

My family fell in love with her the moment they met her. In fact, the night before I left on my very first tour, Dad pulled me aside at our kick off concert and said, "Dan, if you don't marry that girl, I'm gonna take you out back to the woodshed!" There was that imaginary woodshed again.

So, looking back, you can see that my life had some pretty dark moments, with some pretty amazing moments mixed in. Not everything has turned out the way I had hoped. I certainly thought that at this stage of my life, I would have accomplished something, career wise. You know, that one of these artistic endeavors of mine would have found some worldly success.

But I was sitting in the backyard one day of my modest home in Upstate N.Y., a warm summer breeze meeting my face and the intermittent sounds of giggles from the children on our trampoline reaching my ears. My younger son Shea was tooling around on his little four wheeler, zigzagging across our freshly cut lawn, which I had just mowed. Two realizations hit me.

First, one might look at my family and think we must be living the high life. If I had taken a picture right then and there, and put it on Facebook, some might surmise that I was successful - a beautiful big back yard. A trampoline. A four wheeler. Four beautiful children.

However, as with all one dimensional photos, the whole story is never captured on film (or should I say converted into a digital image - c'mon Kulp, get with it!).

You see, the trampoline was given to us by some friends. They bought it a couple years earlier for their two kids, and, as is often the case, it was rarely used. So the mom messaged me one night and asked if I would be interested. Who can pass up a free trampoline? We take it apart and store it in our garage before every winter so that it doesn't rust and look like some of those eyesore models you drive by on occasion.

The four wheeler? Another gift from our wonderful neighbor, Mary. She has grandsons Shea's age. He loves to go over to her house, especially when the grandkids are there. Mary bought two for her grandkids and noticed how much Shea enjoyed riding. And, practically speaking, it is a wonderful little machine for him because, although paralyzed from the waist down, he is able to operate the foot peddle used to propel the ATV, using the weight of his foot and foot brace combined. One day, Mary walked over with a third one and asked if she could keep it in our garage, as she was running out of room in hers. As payment for storage, Shea could use it anytime he liked. That sly devil of a woman! She knew we would feel funny accepting such an exorbitant gift. How crafty. Eventually, she said he could have it. She knew how to ease us into accepting such an awesome gift.

This is the same woman who noticed Shea and I outside on Thanksgiving Day playing in the snow, and, even though she is in her mid-seventies, came over to ask if it would be alright if she had a snowball fight with Shea. I went inside and watched from the warmth of my living room as they hurled white orbs of snow at one another in gleeful fashion.

She is the same neighbor, who, on Christmas morning, dressed up as Santa in full costume (she's a slender lady too, so she really wasn't fooling me or my kids), and hauled a sled with a giant bag of toys for each of our children. God certainly blessed us with wonderful neighbors. On the other side of us are John and Cathy. They may not be as whimsically magical as Mary, but they are equally as generous, kind and considerate.

What if Elizabeth and I faced not only the challenges of our family's special needs, but then had to deal with even one of our neighbors being unkind, mean or belligerent? Worse yet, what if they didn't value our children and their differences or decided we should simply be ignored?

And as for that sprawling back yard? Yes, it seems spacious. We have almost an acre. But what a photo of this particular scene would not reveal is the teeny, tiny house to my back. It's small. We constantly trip over one another and quite frankly, we feel like we are bursting apart at the seams.

People ask, "Hey, how many square feet is your home?" And I'll reply, "Feet?! That would be nice."

Besides great neighbors, another roll of the dice that went my way are my in-laws. Many comedians get great material out of, shall we say, a challenging relationship with either their mother-in-law, father-in-law or both.

No such luck for me. Steve and Kathy Button are great people. Steve is not only like my dad and brother, in that he is another guy in our life who "can fix anything", but he also has their admirable work ethic. Kathy is one of the greatest prayer warriors I have ever known and has been an awesome example of faith to my whole family. Together, they have been extremely supportive and absolutely love their grandkids. Steve is like an overgrown playmate for our kids, and Kathy provides loads of wisdom and nurturing. I can't imagine surviving our sometimes challenging family dynamics without them.

The second truth which occurred to me came from an old post I made on Facebook a couple of years ago. At the time, my mother scolded me for insulting myself. However, it was really meant to be taken the way I hope you take it now. When I wrote and posted it, it was really in a spirit of gratitude, not "woe is me". It went something like this:

"A failed musician. An unknown actor. Unpublished writer and an unsuccessful comedian. An unordained pastor. Overweight, out of shape and balding. Divorced. But when I look at my family, I realize that I am a wealthy, wealthy man. They are my treasure. They are my riches. God has truly blessed me."

And that is how I was feeling on this particular day. Blessed. Wealthy. Satisfied.

In the PBS segment about my family that I mentioned earlier in the book, the last thing my dad said is a quote that I often think of today. Nearing the end of the story, he said, "I was thinking about it the other day, and I realized, I may not be successful out in the business world, but by golly, I feel real successful at home. I really do." Of course he said in one sentence what I needed an entire chapter to tell you. That's my Dad.

21

Dad II

About three hundred people had arrived and packed out the gymnasium in the Pieter's Family Life Center in Henrietta, NY. Since I began writing this book, I've started pastoring a small church (much to my surprise, as well as a lot of other people's, I'm sure). In my mother's wisdom, she declined to have my father's memorial service at my church because she felt there wouldn't be enough space to accommodate all of the people. Mom was right.

Also, the Life Center was close to my dad's heart, as it is owned and operated by Heritage Christian Services. HCS is an incredible organization founded in our hometown of Rochester, NY. They provide the best group homes in the country for the mentally challenged in order to provide residents as much independence as they are capable of, while living life to the fullest. My brothers David and Matthew and sisters Sarah and Suzanne each live in a Heritage house. My mom and dad love the work and ministry they do and offered much support to them over the years. This would be an appropriate place.

While there was the expected shedding of many tears, there was also much joy. Dad had mentioned a couple times over the past year that when he died, he wanted me to do his funeral. It wasn't something I relished and would hastily shrug it off. In the back of my mind, I knew the day would one day come for my father to leave this world, but I hadn't expected it to be anytime soon. One thing I knew was that Mom rightfully wanted it to be a celebration of his life. The other thing I knew was that I had to include humor while balancing it with reverent mourning, all while dealing with my own personal grief.

In early January 2014, I received a call from my mother asking for prayers for Dad. "Why? What is going on?" I asked. Mom explained that he had been diagnosed with lung disease and the doctors thought he might have cancer. He was having trouble breathing and even small amounts of exertion would make him winded. I knew he hadn't been feeling well, but this all came as a surprise. Just the week before, I dropped Emily off to their house and when I arrived, my father had just come in from snow blowing his driveway! He hid his struggle well.

After the news, things seemed to happen pretty fast. Dad was going to various doctor's appointments and eventually had to go to the hospital, where he would remain for almost two months. On his second or third day there, they inserted a breathing tube down his throat. Now he was unable to verbally communicate with us. His condition seemed so severe, I'm not sure he would have been able to anyway. Often he seemed like he was in a coma-like state due to being heavily medicated.

One thing that I am proud of is the way we pulled together as a family. We've always been close, but I think my father's trials in the hospital cemented our bonds even stronger. We made the decision early on to have a family member in his room 24/7, so that whenever he occasionally would awaken, he would see at least one of us by his bedside. Elizabeth and I, my sister Linda and her husband Harvey, and my brother Steve and his wife Ann took rotating shifts which would include two or three overnights at the hospital, along with three or four evening shifts per week, per person. My mother always took the morning and afternoon shifts. My sister Lori, who lives much further away from the area and doesn't drive, would even come for some shifts and also to stay with Mom. We all worked together.

A few weeks in, my father rebounded a bit. The hospital staff was able to sit him up in a chair. He was able to communicate with us using his eyes, hands and even a writing utensil. His upward swing lasted about a week and the decision was made to remove his breathing tube and see how he would do. He did not do well, and soon slid down the road he had been on for so long.

This man, whom as a child I believed was be able to fix anything, was unable to fix his deteriorated lungs.

I was grateful for this week of limited recovery, though. We were able to bring our children to see him and encourage him. Give hugs and kisses. I was able to tell him what a good father he had been. I was at least able to know during this time that he heard me. I considered every moment a gift.

After two months, the time came to have his tube removed for the very last time. My mother so desired to have this done not in the long term care unit which had been his sterile home for the last eight weeks, but in the palliative care unit a few floors below. It was a warmer atmosphere with music and candles, a room with a much homier feeling. Mom had longingly wanted him to leave this world in his own house, but there was no way of making the trip home without killing him. This was the next best option.

We sang "Amazing Grace." Prayed for him. Cried a lot. Read from Romans chapter 8. And, on March 3, 2014, in the afternoon, surrounded by his family, and looking into the devoted and loving eyes of his wife Carol, Norman Carl Kulp peacefully left this world and entered into his eternal home.

His memorial service took place almost two weeks later. The outpouring of love and support was incredible. My best friends and band mates Bill, Mike and Jeff helped to set up tables and chairs and haul sound equipment into the gymnasium. My two other best friends, Tony and Angelo, were also there to help. In addition to many of dad's friends and relatives, members from both my previous church and current church showed up to pay their respects. I was blown away when I saw Dave Hopping, of the comedy duo Dave and Brian, walk through the door. One of my best high school buddies, Lance, a lawyer from State College, PA also came. Both drove around six hours to offer support and neither even knew my father. Mom made the comment about how Dad would have been uncomfortable with all of this. He didn't like crowds and he didn't like to be the center of attention. I truly felt blessed.

My mother and sister requested that I sing "Amazing Grace" and a song called "Sing," written by my friend Jeff and me. Jeff had written the music while I wrote the words back in our days from The DIG Project, and he was now here to accompany me. The gathering also heard music from my great niece, Abby, who performed a flute solo.

One of the most poignant aspects of all of this was the presence of my brothers and sisters with Down syndrome. A lovely woman named Diane Sturmer, from Heritage's Spiritual Care Department, had worked with David, Sarah, Suzanne and Matthew on meaningful ways for them to take part in the service. She also had met with them as a group in order to help them understand what had happened, and to help them express what they felt about it.

Prior to the service, they all contributed to a picture displaying their ideas about "Dad's Home in Heaven". He was in a huge house. The home had the name of all of his kids and sons and daughters-in-law with a smiley face under each name. There was a cookbook, as Dad loved to cook and was an excellent chef. A pot of coffee. Pasta and Dad's favorite food – pizza! In front of his new home were a row of flowers – another favorite of Dad's. He had quite a green thumb. And there was a Buffalo Bills flag flying in the yard. Oh yeah, and there was Dad, with a huge smile on his face.

Once at the service, Suzanne said a prayer. Sarah used some sign language to express herself. Matthew handed out bulletins. David surprised everyone by standing up during a time of sharing. He spoke about how much he missed his father and through many tears, pointed out all of the rest of the family members one by one by name. He seemed to take Dad's passing harder than the rest, but expressed his loss in such a beautiful way.

Three planned speakers commenced with thoughts about Dad before we opened the floor for anyone who wanted to have a chance to share a memory. One of my father's close friends, Al, spoke, followed by my wife, then my brother, Steve. All were inspiring. After the open floor with a few friends and family members adding remembrances, it was my turn to deliver a sermon.

Like I said, Dad had mentioned a few times over the past year that "someday" he wanted me to do his funeral. I would quickly brush him off and changed the subject. Fathers are forever, don't you know? Now, the time had come. When he had first told me about lung cancer possibly taking up residence in his seventy-six year old chest, the reality hit me when I arrived home and told my wife. Breaking down in tears, I said, "He's going to want me to do his funeral." The thought seemed devastating. I wasn't sure how I would grieve and conduct a memorial service at the same time. It all seemed overwhelming.

Here it was, a couple months later and I was ready to deliver. I spoke about how much he and I were alike. Family was of utmost importance, up near the top of the list when it comes to priorities; that was one of the major lessons I had learned from him. I even told a couple of jokes, which I knew he would enjoy. I spoke about the legacy he left for me to follow with my own family. I told of his faith in Jesus Christ and my faith in the fact that Dad was now with Him in paradise.

Soon, the celebration of his life was over, and Dad was not here.

Remember when I mentioned how my mother was probably the driving force behind their adoptions of David, Suzanne and Sarah? About a year before Dad passed, long before he was even sick, I read an early draft of the book to the both of them, specifically the chapters about my mother. I was anxious to have them hear what I wrote. When I got to that statement about Mom being the driving force, her eyebrow raised and she gave a look like maybe I wasn't completely accurate. She explained that Dad was a bit of a softy and would get his heart strings pulled by mere pictures of children who needed parents. I didn't realize this fact, but it was later reinforced by my sister, Lori, when we were gathered at Dad's bedside in the hospital. Laughing, she said, "I love the story about how Dad got sick and they ended up with Sarah."

"What do you mean"? I asked.

She told of a time when Dad called into work sick with a cold, and to pass the time at home, he began to flip through the pages of something which was quite a big deal in our home. It was called the C.A.P. (Council of Adoptive Parents) Book. He saw a picture of Sarah and felt he and Mom were meant to be her parents. Now I love that story, too.

Thinking back to chapter one, as I was sitting in that restaurant, I realized I received two incredible gifts during my time in China. The first great gift was obviously my son Simon. I thought at my age I had experienced every emotion there was to feel. Simon awoke in me brand new emotions that I never realized existed deep down in my soul. He changed my life in a way I never dreamed possible. My little buddy Simon says "I love you" in a hundred different ways, all without uttering a single word. However, it is not only his love for me which causes my heart to stir. But when I first went from being childless to becoming a father, I was awestruck by the great love I had for him. I never would have realized I had the capacity to love to this great depth.

Before you say, "Hey, what about your wife? What is she? Chopped liver?" and attempt to get me in all sorts of hot water, let me just say that my love for my wife is different. It is not shallow or without profundity, it's just that it is so mutual. We love each other. We offer one another satisfying benefits to being a husband and wife. We are two independent people who, separately, were able to take care of ourselves, and each made the choice to commit our lives to one another. So, while I love her and owe to her my life and the story which I now live, it is just plain different than being a dad. And, unlike my wife, my children can never understand the depth of my love for them.

My kids do not understand the following:

- There is nothing they can do to change the fact that I love them.

- There is nowhere they can run to where I won't run after them.

- There is nowhere I wouldn't go just to be with them.

- There is no dark doorway I would not enter to find them.

- I would give up everything I have and everything I am ever going to have, if I must, to have them in my life.

- I will do anything for them, except for those things that in my wisdom I know shouldn't be done for them.

- There is nothing I wouldn't give them, except for those things I know they shouldn't have. But I will always look for and desire to give them something better to replace that which I withhold.

- I would gladly take upon my own shoulders any weight they couldn't handle.

- I would take their sickness, hurts, pains, heartaches and sadness if I could.

- I will mourn when they mourn and rejoice when they rejoice.

- If for some reason I had to die for them, I would. Take a bullet, a sword, and if I had to stand between them and the Grim Reaper himself, I would. Always.

- I will toil, struggle, sweat and work to protect and provide for them all the days of my life.

- I will never ever leave them or forsake them.

- They are always on my mind.

My kids will never understand this. All they can conceive is that Daddy loves them (see chapter 19). And all I desire from them is that they respond to my love.

The second great gift I received during my first trip to China was that, for two weeks, I got to experience just a taste of what my father experienced here in our country back in the seventies and eighties. I realized then, as people stared at us and whispered to one another about us and questioned why in the world we would want a child who was "different", that for two whole weeks I got to feel just a bit of what he must have felt. This man who hated attention and standing out in a crowd, and yet would often have a spotlight of attention shone on him. This man would rather have blended in and mixed into the background, yet would endure all of this for the love of his family. Yes, for two weeks I got to follow in my father's footsteps. And that is a gift I wouldn't trade for anything in the world. For two whole weeks, I got to be like Dad.

Heroes

Often people will say something to me like, "Adopting children with special needs is quite a calling," or "It's so nice you and your wife responded to God's calling to adopt."

I've come to realize, though, that it is not a calling. Adoption is a choice. God tells us to take care of orphans. He makes that mandate very clear in Scripture. So you choose to either adopt or you don't. You see, I think many people choose to refer to this gift of adoption as a calling in order to let themselves off the hook from choosing to adopt an orphan. Deep down many people think, "It's a calling, and well, I don't feel called, so I don't have to adopt. But it sure is nice those other people over there are called."

No, it's a choice.

Do you think God would be angry with anyone for making that choice? Think of things we do all the time without ever even consulting God or bringing it to Him in prayer. We purchase cars. Use credit cards. Take out loans. Build pools. Go back to school. Date, marry and break up. We spend time and money on hobbies. Buy big screen TV's. Rehearse with our bands and play golf. Yet, when it comes to saving the life of a child, many tell themselves they would have to have some sort of mysterious, magical, angelic light appear with a voice like James Earl Jones saying, "Hence, I say go forth and bring thou one of My littlest into your abode and raise them up in My steadfast and ever abiding love". Let me make it easy for you. You don't even have to pray about it. God is OK with you making this choice.

Don't get me wrong. There may be some circumstances for which you might not be truly able or ready to make this choice. So you choose not to. Just realize it for what it is.

Every baby killed in an abortion clinic is done so out of convenience. In case you think I misspoke here, I'll say it again. Every baby killed in an abortion clinic is done so out of convenience.

But you say, "Dan! What if the mother doesn't have the money to raise a child?" It's quite inconvenient to work harder in life or sell possessions or go without the perks that others may enjoy in order to support another human being.

"Well, what if the mother is still in school, or hasn't gone to college yet?" Yes, very inconvenient to have to delay our own dreams and ambitions for the sake of another human being.

And, the mack daddy of all pro-abortion arguments, "What about rape or incest?" Based on the extreme emotional trauma caused by such brutal and sickening acts, it could be a huge emotional toll on a woman to carry a child for nine months as a daily reminder of what she endured. And, thus, would be very inconvenient.

But, let me say, the same thing can be said for every choice made by a person to not adopt a child who needs parents. The choice is most likely made out of convenience. I understand you may be way too old or have some physical condition preventing you from adopting. But if not, as a pro-life Christian ask yourself, "Am I guilty of the same type of thinking as the pro-abortion crowd by acting (or not acting) out of convenience?" What if every Christian couple adopted an orphan? There would be no orphan problem. Think about it.

At the very least, please consider some alternatives: become a foster parent; sponsor a child through Christian relief organizations like World Vision or Compassion International; start a clothing or fund drive for orphans and foster children in your community; provide respite for adoptive or foster parents; make or collect needed orphanage supplies (like shoes, medicine, etc.); go on a short term mission trip and work in overseas orphanages; donate to orphan care ministries like Reece's Rainbow; advocate for children waiting to be adopted; or provide acts of service for a family you know who have taken that step of faith down the road of adoption.

I promise, somewhere in the world, there is a child waiting for somebody just like you to act on their behalf.

I knew what I wanted to be when I grew up. As a kid with undiagnosed ADD (my mom can verify, and mostly likely you can, too, now that you've seen how I write), I figured that being an actor would allow me to be everything – an astronaut, cowboy, cop or even Elvis! But, more than any of those, I longed to be a superhero. I thought I could actually grow up to be independently wealthy and have a secret cave somewhere with all the latest high tech equipment. From there, I would be able to fight crime and rid the world of evil.

As I matured (not as easily verifiable), my view of what a superhero actually is evolved. It shifted from the polyester pajama-wearing, cape donning masked men of seventies TV shows to people like my parents. Norm and Carol Kulp made the choice to adopt three children with Down syndrome, adding to the one they already had, despite a culture which said these children should be put into institutions and forgotten about. They battled the currents of bigotry and ignorance for the glory of love (insert Peter Cetera song here).

My superheroes also became my brothers and sisters, as well as all those with special needs who get up every day, usually with a smile on their face and love in their heart, and choose to take on the world and all of its challenges in ways you and I could never possibly imagine.

People like my wife also became my heroes. Elizabeth saw an injustice in the world and made the choice to do something about it. She not only determined in her heart to get an orphan out of a deadly place, but by telling others about her experiences, she has inspired them to make the same choice.

You know who else I can put into the heroes category? Our friends Jeff and Joey Norsen. Remember that couple we psyched out by getting them interested in adopting Shea, and then adopted him ourselves? Well, God certainly knew the whole time about other plans He had for them. They ended up taking in a foster child, which led to her adoption. Then, they took in another child who, which you guessed it, they adopted! Foster parents are big heroes in my book, as it takes a lot of strength to take in children you might have to say goodbye to after a while. But it is so needed for the lives of these kids.

The men and women who fight everyday on behalf of the unborn are my heroes too. For example, those who choose to work or volunteer for Pregnancy Care Centers. They minister to young mothers with nowhere to turn, fathers who feel ill equipped to take care of their families, and babies who need a chance. They fight because they understand that life is valuable.

I have the joy and the privilege of speaking at Pregnancy Care Center fundraisers all over the country to help them raise money to do their life-saving work. I take it all very personally. Every time people choose to open their checkbooks and give to their work, it feels like someone is telling me that my son, a little boy left in the woods on December 28, 2004 in the middle of winter, with snow beginning to cover his little body, well, it feels like someone has said, "Your son's life is valuable. He is worth fighting for."

Like me being able to follow in my dad's footsteps, we are all given that opportunity, aren't we? We all are able to follow in our Heavenly Father's footsteps. Each time we value another human being, adopt a child, do foster care, reach out to a child with special needs, fight for those who can't fight for themselves, we are walking the path that Jesus Christ walked. Thank you Mom, Dad and Elizabeth for showing me where to put my feet.

Epilogue

Almost one year has passed. The Kulp family is still getting used to the absence of our patriarch. Since my father's death on March 3, 2014, we have gone through a Father's Day, my parent's anniversary, Mom's birthday, Dad's birthday, Thanksgiving, Christmas and the start of a new year without him here. Usually he would sit in his same living room chair and pass out good-natured ribbing to each of us as we entered the room on these celebratory occasions. For the past year, the chair has remained empty.

All of us are still adjusting. For Mom, this couldn't be truer. How could it not be? They were married for almost 60 years. Her house is empty. Her husband, friend, companion, lover and partner is gone. My mother's strength and dignity shines as bright now, though, as it did when I was growing up.

As I travel and perform, people often approach me afterwards and ask what my brothers and sisters are doing now that they are adults. For a while, I was proudly answering, "Oh, they are each in their own group home." I was sometimes met with strange looks, not realizing that in some parts of the country, "group home" are dirty words to the special needs community. They can represent not so nice places where the mentally or physically challenged are placed and forgotten about and or treated coldly by the staff.

For David, Sarah, Suzanne and Matthew, their experience is profoundly different. We have Heritage Christian Services to thank for that. Heritage provides homes all throughout the Rochester and Buffalo areas, and they are top notch. My brothers and sisters are surrounded by their friends and some of the finest staff I have ever seen in the field of developmental challenges. Each of them has a very active social calendar, a job, and they take better vacations than I do. In Rochester, we have a minor league baseball team called the Rochester Red Wings. I have to laugh, because I only make it to about one game per year, and at the last three, I bumped into my brother Matthew, who was there with his buddies from his house.

There is a lengthy waiting list for people to get into one of these houses and as a family, we count ourselves blessed that my siblings are all in. It was my parent's strong desire for each of them to be in a Heritage home because they wanted to be sure that as all of us get older, no matter what happened, the four of them would be taken care of. David was the last one to make it. In fact, a representative went to the hospital when my father was there to tell him David had been accepted into a Heritage Christian Home. Taking care of his family had always been my dad's top priority. In his final weeks, he could know that he and my mother had succeeded yet again.

Elizabeth still practices physical therapy part time for homebound patients. I'm proud of her and how great she is at what she does. I'm even more proud of how she takes such incredible care of our children. She tends to their complex medical needs, handles all of our insurance issues, appointments and scheduling, advocating for our children with the school district, and being a wonderful mother and wife. I marvel at her ability to do it all with such grace and love.

Simon is one of the happiest kids I know. He loves to jump, and play with his stuffed animals and electronic toys. Like his introverted father, he's very content having alone time. I've mentioned how Simon was a Daddy's boy. At ten years old, however, he seems to have become more balanced in his affection towards both Elizabeth and I. No problem with me, as he has more than enough love to spread around. He has a very limited vocabulary and is considered non-verbal. I've been writing a song about Simon for the last few years, some of the lyrics include: *"Simon says I love you without a single word, and when I say 'I love you, too', I know that I've been heard"*.

Danielle loves her role as big sister. She loves to help with her siblings and especially likes to help in the kitchen. Setting the table, getting drinks out and washing dishes thrill her. She's also the best egg cracker I have ever seen, rarely getting a shell in the eggs. She likes to watch the same movie every day for about three months before moving on to another. These movies usually involve a lot of singing. For a while it was "Pete's Dragon", then a VeggieTales movie, then a Muppet movie, and then "Annie." Now, it's the movie "Frozen." I really can't wait until she is ready to "Let it go, let it go". On Fridays, Danielle plays on a basketball team for children with special needs. When I attend her practices, I feel sort of like I did when I'd go to the Christmas service for people with mental and physical challenges at the Presbyterian Church. Close to God.

Shea is a jock. He loves sports. If he could play soccer, football, hockey and baseball he would, and I have no doubt he would excel. For now, he has really taken to his Rookies team for children and teens who use wheelchairs. He even went to his first regional competition last summer. In the fall, he raced in a 5K for charity, alongside Ryan Chalmers and a teen named Chase, whom Shea looks up to. Ryan, the son of Shea's coach, is a young man who made headlines for pushing his racing chair over 3,000 miles across the country to raise money and awareness for charity. Shea is also involved with Boy Scouts. In fact, last weekend he took second place for most creative car in the Pinewood Derby. I've always been impressed with his advanced communication abilities. I think Shea could charm anyone and often does. I won't be surprised if one day he works in a field which requires public speaking and strong people skills.

When I wrote the chapter about Emily, I expressed how easy going she is, and how she "goes with the flow." Well, she is three years old now and has become an explosion of energy – loud, boisterous and energetic. She runs, jumps, dances, sings and performs constantly. She has a loud voice like mine and definitely makes it heard. Emily can be a little princess one moment and a tomboy the next. She adores each of her siblings. I still say God gave us the perfect biological child to fit our family. Although, as Elizabeth points out, Emily is often our most challenging one. And, yes, she has Dad wrapped around her little finger.

One of the traits which all four of my children share is an incredible sense of humor. I don't want to leave you with the impression that everything is smooth sailing all of the time for the Kulp household. That couldn't be further from the truth. Elizabeth and I are tired most of the time. Between medical appointments and procedures, and balancing home and work, we feel constantly on the run and a little overwhelmed. But laughter really is good medicine. I'm delighted that each family member has a very distinct sense of humor and uses it regularly. We laugh a lot, just like the family I grew up with. Emily sometimes asks, "Daddy, do I make you laugh?" She does.

They all do.

I am still feeling blessed.

Photo courtesy of George Eastman House

Shea in his first 5K.

Acknowledgments

For a writer, this must be one of the scariest parts of writing a book. I have to now think back and try and remember every single person who helped me, not just with this book, but with every little aspect of my life who contributed to me getting in the right place to write this book. There have been many, so I fear leaving someone off the list of acknowledgments someone who should be acknowledged. I apologize in advance. If you believe I should have included you and didn't, please forgive me. So that you won't hold it against me or so that things are not awkward the next time I see you, I offer you this: Upon informing me of my error, I will publicly apologize on Facebook and acknowledge your contribution there. If it is any consolation to you, nobody reads the acknowledgments anyway. At best, they scan them. A Facebook post will get a lot more traffic and hopefully, you will feel you received the recognition you deserve.

Obviously, the first person to mention has to be my wife Elizabeth. If I didn't, I would be the scourge of every woman who made it to the end of this book. Now, by listing Elizabeth as numero uno, I've just received a whole bunch of "awww"s from my female readership. So here it goes: Elizabeth, every time I walked out the door to go someplace and work on this story, it was you who had the harder work of having "kid duty" at home, by yourself. To say I couldn't have done this without you is an understatement. I wouldn't have nearly the story to tell if it wasn't for you coming home from China that first time and sharing yours. I love that God has made it "our story". Favorite memory from this process? The time we got away to Skaneateles for a couple of days and I read the entire manuscript to you and you helped me fix what needed to be fixed and improve what needed to be improved and remember what needed to be remembered. I love you and am so grateful God brought us together to be not only soul mates, but also teammates in this adventure called parenthood. (Can I hear an "Awwww"?)

Simon, Danielle, Shea and Emily, you are the loves of my life.

Mom and Dad, I can't thank you enough for your legacy. I am grateful every day for you choosing to adopt my brother David and sisters Suzanne and Sarah. My life never would have been the same without them. Much like my wife, the reason I have a story to tell is because of your story and how you instilled in me the value of life, adoption and the joy of people with special needs. Thanks, too, for always believing in me. I can remember when I sheepishly told you I was hitting the road on my first tour with the band. It seemed absurd. I mean, I was thirty-three years old and was giving up income, a place to live and pursuing something that most started in their early twenties. Mom, I'll never forget how, when I told you all of this, you looked at me and said, "It's about time!" I suppose it is that same belief in me that gave me the audacity to write a book. Thank you from the bottom of my heart.

Steven Curtis and Mary Beth Chapman, words are not enough to express what I feel in my heart for what you have given to me and my family. Without you, we never would have had this bright, joyful light in our lives whom we call Simon. I am confident there are thousands of other parents who would echo my gratitude.

David, Suzanne, Sarah and Matthew – There aren't enough pages to describe what you have given me or how my life would have been different if I had never been introduced to the joy of Down syndrome through you. Thanks for being such great brothers and sisters and for your unconditional love.

Other family members Linda and Harvey, Steve and Ann, Lori and Joe, Chris, Josh and Andrea and my numerous nieces and nephews – big thanks.

Steve and Kathy Button, thank you for being such great in-laws and grandparents. Oh, and thanks for letting me marry your hot daughter.

Bill Griffin, Mike Higgins, Jeff Norsen – my band mates. Let's be honest, you didn't help me with this at all. However, you've helped me with life for the past fifteen years. We met during my darkest hour, and you have celebrated with me at the best of times. You are my brothers and I love you.

When the band stopped touring, I had no idea what I was going to do with my life. Comedians Dave Hopping and Brian Smith, you led me down the road of comedy as a career path. How many times have I opened up for you and totally sucked? Yet, you kept on asking. Thanks for seeing something inside me long before 1 or others did. Being in your videos is the highlight of my acting career, too.

Walking beside us for all three of our adoptions and the birth of Emily was our former church family of Farmington

UMC. Thank you for your fellowship, friendship, and financial and emotional support.

I sometimes wonder if the First Baptist Church of Manchester wonders what they got themselves into. They hired a traveling comedian, actor and rock singer instead of an ordained seminary graduate to be their minister. You put up with my travels, family obligations and lack of credentials. As one of my spiritual heroes, Mike Yaconelli, referred to himself, you got yourself a "K-mart pastor". Thanks for bringing to me a whole new set of experiences to continue my story.

Show Hope, Reece's Rainbow, Andrea Roberts, Flower City Down Syndrome Network, Never Say Never Foundation, Wayne ARC, Rochester Rookies, Holy Childhood – I can't even begin to express my gratitude for you.

To my friends Jason Jurewicz, Tony Montone, Angelo Diminuco and Kerry Colling – thanks for your friendship.

I have what I consider to be two spiritual mentors whom I am intensely grateful for their guidance and leadership over the years – TK and Pastor Jeff.

This falls under the "I hope I don't forget somebody who's feelings will be hurt if I forget to include them". I really can't justify thanking my old high school friends Lance Marshall, Doug Reinholtz and Shawn Greer, other than I love them and wanted to tell them so in print.

Fellow comedians Derrick Tennant, Gordon Douglas, Mike Williams, Paul Aldrich, Jonny Wethington and Brad Stine

Thanks to my high school choir director and voice teacher, Christine Sargent. Even though she didn't have anything to do with this, let's face it. When will I ever write a book about my singing career? So, thanks for teaching me how to sing, Sarge.

Thanks to all the brave, young ladies who babysit or have babysat for us on a regular basis – Katie, Kendra, Margarita, Andrea, Mrs. Socha, Mary Alice, Hannah, Amanda, Rachel, the Phillips girls, Vicki, Linda, Ann Marie and Simon's special buddy, Carli. (Notice there aren't any dudes courageous enough?).

I am so appreciative of the special education teachers, bus drivers, therapists and aides who work with and place so much value on our children.

Nurse Anne, Nurse Renee, and Nurse Vonda - incredibly grateful for your care towards our children.

Gloria, Dana, Sara, Maria, Emily, Sherry and Wes at Ambassador Speakers Bureau – Thank you for booking for me and partnering with me to spread this message of life.

Thank you Joanne Brokaw. You got me my first paid writing gig doing film reviews, work that most of my friends and family thought was the perfect job for me due to my passion for film. I'm also grateful for connecting me with a publisher, for your encouragement every step of the way, and for making me a better writer. I hope this sells a bazillion copies so that you get some sort of compensation commensurate with your hard work.

Mike Parker, I don't know you, but I think we are kindred spirits. Thanks for publishing this thing! (I know you think exclamation points are overused, so that one was for you).

Wordcrafts, thanks for publishing this thing!

NOTES on QUOTES

Page 98 *President of the United States made a mockery ... "like the Special Olympics or something"* - March 19th, 2009 The Tonight Show with Jay Leno

http://abcnews.go.com/blogs/politics/2009/03/president-ob-15-3/

Page 100 *Al Gore attacked supporters of Oliver North "...the extreme right wing, the extra chromosome right wing."* - "Election 94: North Rips Gore For Attack On Backers" Daily Press, October 29, 2004

http://articles.dailypress.com/1994-10-30/news/9410300010_1_north-s-campaign-charles-robb-coal-miner

Page 101 *"If they have a misshapen lamb, they get rid of it... smashed against the wall and be dealt with."* - Felicity Morse, "Disability Rights: Cornish Councillor Colin Brewer Compares Disabled Children To Deformed Lambs", Huffington Post UK, November 5, 2013

http://www.huffingtonpost.co.uk/2013/05/11/cornish-councillor-disability-colin-brewer-deformed-lambs-_n_3259240.html

Page 102 *"The object of civilization is to obtain the highest and most splendid culture of which humanity is capable... impede progress and ever increasingly drag down the human race."* The Public Writing and Speeches of Margaret Sanger website

http://www.nyu.edu/projects/sanger/webedition/app/documents/show.php?sangerDoc=306638.xml

Page 102 *In his quest ... Operation T-4 euthanasia program before moving on to the Jews.* Jewish Virtual Library

http://www.jewishvirtuallibrary.org/jsource/Holocaust/disabled.html

Resources

Autism Society
The nation's leading grassroots autism organization exists to improve the lives of all affected by autism by increasing public awareness about the day-to-day issues faced by people on the spectrum; advocating for appropriate services for individuals across the lifespan; and providing the latest information regarding treatment, education, research and advocacy.
www.autism-society.org/

Care Net Pregnancy Centers
Care Net's mission is to provide compassion, hope, and help to women and men facing pregnancy decisions. Through their network of affiliated centers and real-time Pregnancy Decision Coaching call center, they present realistic alternatives to abortion so people will choose life for their unborn children and abundant life for their families.
www.care-net.org/

Chromosome 9pminus Network (Alfi's syndrome):
A nonprofit, parent-based support group with a mission to improve the lives of families affected by 9p Deletion Syndrome by connecting families, offering knowledge, and improving access to information about this rare genetic disorder.
www.9pminus.org

Compassion International
Christian child advocacy ministry that releases children from spiritual, economic, social and physical poverty and enables them to become responsible, fulfilled Christian adults.
www.compassion.com/

Heartbeat International
Heartbeat's life-saving mission is to reach and rescue as many lives as possible, around the world, through an effective network of pregnancy help ministries that renew their communities for life.
www.heartbeatinternational.org/

Heritage Christian Services
For more than thirty years, Heritage Christian Services has been serving people with developmental disabilities in Monroe, Wayne, Livingston, Erie and Niagara counties in New York State through residential support, day programs, service coordination, respite, community habilitation, employment supports and licensed home care services.
www.heritagechristianservices.org/

National Down Syndrome Congress
Provides information, advocacy and support concerning all aspects of life for individuals with Down syndrome, and works to create a national climate in which all people will recognize and embrace the value and dignity of people with Down syndrome.
www.ndsccenter.org/

National Down Syndrome Society
The mission of the National Down Syndrome Society is to be the national advocate for the value, acceptance and inclusion of people with Down syndrome.
www.ndss.org

Never Say Never Foundation

Not-for-profit organization located in Webster, N.Y. providing equine-assisted activities and educational experiences to children of all abilities through services and programs, such as camps, educational field trips, and special events.
www.nsnstables.org/

Reece's Rainbow

The mission of Reece's Rainbow is to advocate and find families for orphans with Down syndrome and other special needs by raising funds for adoption grants and promoting awareness through an online community, media communications, and other events.
www.reecesrainbow.org

Show Hope

Founded by Steven Curtis Chapman and his wife Mary Beth, this nonprofit organization is helping to make a difference for the millions of orphans and waiting children around the world.
www.showhope.org

Special Olympics

A global movement of people creating a new world of inclusion and community, where every single person is accepted and welcomed, regardless of ability or disability.
www.specialolympics.org/

Spina Bifida Association

SBA is the only national voluntary health agency solely dedicated to enhancing the lives of those with Spina Bifida and those whose lives are touched by this challenging birth defect. Its tools are education, advocacy, research and service.
www.spinabifidaassociation.org

World Vision
Christian humanitarian organization dedicated to working with children, families and their communities worldwide to reach their full potential by tackling the causes of poverty and injustice.
www.worldvision.org/

About Dan & Elizabeth Kulp

Dan shares his humor at banquets, conferences, schools, colleges, seminars, churches, camps and anywhere else people would like to have him. He would be honored to come for your group.

For booking, please contact Ambassador Speakers Bureau

615.370.4700 or **info@ambassadorspeakers.com**

You may also correspond with the author at **dan@thedigproject.com**

For more about Dan Kulp and his family, including videos, photos, links and other extras, visit: **www.kulponline.com/**

Elizabeth Kulp blogs about daily life in the Kulp household at: **www.thekulpchronicles.blogspot.com/**

To watch the 1980 PBS/Newsweek documentary "Adoption in America", featuring the Kulp family, visit: **www.youtube.com/watch?v=SZAC9-g88Os**

To see Dan and Elizabeth's inspirational adoption video Somebody Just Like You, please go to: **www.youtube.com/watch?v=lYLqaQMZdpU**

Also Available From

WordCrafts Press

Morning Mist
Stories from the Water's Edge
by Barbie Loflin

Why I Failed in the Music Business
and how NOT to follow in my footsteps
by Steve Grossman

Youth Ministry is Easy!
and 9 other lies
by Aaron Shaver

Chronicles of a Believer
by Don McCain

Illuminations
by Paula K. Parker & Tracy Sugg

Pro-Verb Ponderings
31 Ruminations on Positive Action
by Rodney Boyd

www.wordcrafts.net

Made in the USA
Middletown, DE
21 February 2022

61493213R00106